T0271409

Social Brand Management in a Post Covid-19 Era

As activity significantly reduced during mandatory lockdown periods aiming to contain the spread of Covid-19, the relationship between organizations and their stakeholders became almost strictly digital. While some brands already have developed digital channels and made a smooth transition, others struggled to remain connected to their consumers and in the process created a panoply of new digital strategies and practices. This book discusses how the Covid-19 pandemic changed the way consumers relate with brands and how brands can reinvent, improve, or optimize themselves to meet new needs, expectations, and preferences of consumers.

Drawing on empirical data about how consumers are connecting with brands in a Covid-19 recovery period, this book suggests becoming a social brand as a strategy for coping with changes in consumer behaviour. A social brand has two main dimensions: it is sociable (active on social media, humanized, and empathic) and it is socially committed (transparent and sustainable). In this concise book, the authors examine case studies of brands that coped successfully with Covid-19 and positioned themselves strongly in this post-pandemic retake period to suggest good practices. It offers an informed discussion on how brands can adapt to changes in consumer behaviour and build stronger connections with consumers.

Social Brand Management in a Post Covid-19 Era provides an accessible yet comprehensive overview of brand management in a post-pandemic environment that will be of interest to marketing and communication academics, researchers, and students.

Patrícia Dias is an Assistant Professor at Universidade Católica Portuguesa and a Researcher at CECC – Research Centre for Communication and Culture and CRC-W – Católica Research Centre in Psychology, Family and Social Wellbeing.

Alexandre Duarte is an Assistant Professor at Universidade NOVA de Lisboa, an Invited Professor at Universidade Católica Portuguesa, and a Researcher at ICNOVA – Universidade Nova de Lisboa

Routledge Focus on Business and Management

The fields of business and management have grown exponentially as areas of research and education. This growth presents challenges for readers trying to keep up with the latest important insights. *Routledge Focus on Business and Management* presents small books on big topics and how they intersect with the world of business.

Individually, each title in the series provides coverage of a key academic topic, whilst collectively, the series forms a comprehensive collection across the business disciplines.

Pop-Up Retail
The Evolution, Application and Future of Ephemeral Stores
Ghalia Boustani

Building Virtual Teams
Trust, Culture, and Remote Work
Catalina Dumitru

Fostering Wisdom at Work
Jeff M. Allen

Artificial Intelligence, Business and Civilization
Our Fate Made in Machines
Andreas Kaplan

Power in Business Relationships
Dynamics, Strategies and Internationalisation
Dariusz Siemieniako, Maciej Mitręga, Hannu Makkonen and Gregor Pfajfar

For more information about this series, please visit: www.routledge.com/ Routledge-Focus-on-Business-and-Management/book-series/FBM

Social Brand Management in a Post Covid-19 Era

Patrícia Dias and Alexandre Duarte (coords.)

Disclaimer:
This volume was financed through a national endowment by FCT – Fundação para a Ciência e Tecnologia – as part of project ref. no. UIDB/00126/2020 | UIDP/00126/2020

Routledge
Taylor & Francis Group

LONDON AND NEW YORK

CATOLICA
CECC · RESEARCH CENTRE FOR COMMUNICATION AND CULTURE

LISBOA

Fundação
para a Ciência
e a Tecnologia

UIDB/00126/2020 | UIDP/00126/2020

First published 2023
by Routledge
4 Park Square, Milton Park, Abingdon, Oxon OX14 4RN

and by Routledge
605 Third Avenue, New York, NY 10158

Routledge is an imprint of the Taylor & Francis Group, an informa business

© 2023 Patrícia Dias and Alexandre Duarte

The right of Patrícia Dias and Alexandre Duarte to be identified as authors of this work has been asserted in accordance with sections 77 and 78 of the Copyright, Designs and Patents Act 1988.

Trademark notice: Product or corporate names may be trademarks or registered trademarks, and are used only for identification and explanation without intent to infringe.

British Library Cataloguing-in-Publication Data
A catalogue record for this book is available from the British Library

ISBN: 978-1-032-46572-2 (hbk)
ISBN: 978-1-032-46573-9 (pbk)
ISBN: 978-1-003-38233-1 (ebk)

DOI: 10.4324/9781003382331

Typeset in Times New Roman
by codeMantra

Contents

Introduction

We are witnessing a time of accelerated change, and, as the father of social psychology Kurt Lewin wisely observed, the best moment to study a social phenomenon is when it is in the process of change, as it is when an entity is in movement and alteration that its dynamics are revealed more clearly. This is the main reason for the publishing of this book right now.

We live in a world of mass consumption, where everything can be branded, from a soap to a car, from a mobile phone to a hospital, from water to a football player. This book starts, therefore, with a trip to the foundations of brands. How they appear? What are they? What they represent?

Brands are promises of satisfaction. They are signs, metaphors that act like a non-written contract between the offer of a company, many times intangible, and the stakeholders for whom it aims to reach.

That way, this book tries to give a step forward in terms of the symbolism that brands represent now-a-days, looking at them as part of the culture in which they exist and express all its meanings, while trying to conceptualize a new construct that we've defined as Social Brands.

Divided in five chapters, which one written by a reputed author, the journey around brands and branding is made focusing on the relation between its essence and the stakeholders who it is concerned to, paying special attention to the changes that have occurred because of the Covid-19 pandemic.

The first chapter looks to the relationship between brands and consumers, discussing the most important milestones in the evolution of this concepts and the emergence of the branding construct. Finally, it reviews the role of brands in an ever-increasing polarized world, where consumers demand companies to dialogue and maintain a para-social relation with them and to take a stance in critical social issues, forcing brands to stand a position in several controversial themes, assuming, therefore, a social positioning.

Given this kickoff, the second chapter addresses how Covid-19 has changed this dynamic relationship between brands and their audiences. Analyzing the publics, how they faced all this problematic, and how brand dealt with it, especially through institutional communication. This chapter ends looking

DOI: 10.4324/9781003382331-1

into the case study of the University of Minho and their crisis communication during the pandemic time, from the point of view of a social brand concept.

In the third part, we turn our attention to the successful formulas that brands have used to deal with Covid-19. Several examples are shown, explained, and analyzed, such as Spotify, Airbnb, or Cata Vassalo. Humanization and attention to experience and empathy are highlighted as strengths of some of the brands that stood out in this period.

Our journey continues in the fourth chapter, which starts looking into the digital realm, the human characteristics such as imagination and ambition, and how all these items are combined to contribute to shape human evolution. This chapter finishes by raising some critical issues that brands will face in this post-Covid 19 period, providing crucial answers for better understanding the future of brands.

Finally, the last chapter gathers all previous discussed concepts and points to the attempt to define a concept of Social Brands. Looking to the relationship between the digital environment, the social context, the demands of the new consumers, and the role of the firms, the challenges and opportunities for brands are discussed. In short, it explains how, in contemporary times, to stand out and matter, brands should become Social Brands.

1 The relationship between brands and consumers

Alexandre Duarte

ICNOVA/Universidade Nova de Lisboa

This first chapter begins with an overview of the concept of brands. It discusses its evolution and key milestones in the branding literature, analyzing the role of brands both from the companies' perspective and in the lives of consumers.

In the second part, this chapter focuses on the consumer, not only his new reality, power, needs, and desires but also his demands, especially in his relationship with brands in this new paradigm in which brands are seen as a social process that emerges from the permanent interactions between all stakeholders.

Finally, political and social consumerism is discussed, where the concepts of corporate social responsibility, corporate activism, and social positioning (both for companies and for consumers) are at the center of the debate and a fundamental part of where the concept of social brands is based.

1.1 A brand new world or a new brand world?

> Two-thirds of the globe is covered by water.
> The rest is covered by brands.

This quote is not as exaggerated as it might seem at first glance. Indeed, it seems that brands and their persuasive communication surround us almost permanently wherever we look. According to Lee and Heere (2018), it is estimated that each individual is in touch with anywhere between 3,000 and 20,000 commercial messages a day. Of course, humans have no possible cognitive capacity to analyze and interpret this gigantic mountain of marketing information to which all the other personal, cultural, religious, political, sports, news, etc. information is added. However, when does the brand phenomenon it started?

In English, the word "brand" comes from the archaic Scandinavian with a Germanic root, "brandr", which means "to burn" (Khan & Mufti, 2007; Healey, 2009), anything that was hot or burning, such as a piece of "firemark" (Rajaram & Shelly, 2012, p.100). In fact, the brand phenomenon is very old, and its proof can be found in the places where cattle were usually sold, and

DOI: 10.4324/9781003382331-2

the sellers burn specific symbols on their own animals. So, to brand something can literally be understood when we talk about marking the cattle or a barrel of whiskey, for instance, to indicate its owner. And figuratively, when we talk about all the attributes of a product leaving a lasting impression in our memory.

According to Ruão (2006), the first forms of brands emerged in Lydia in the year 700 BC, when merchants placed hired people at the door of their commercial establishments to proclaim the characteristics and advantages of their products as a way of attracting customers. As for the Romans, one of the techniques that proved to be most effective was the paintings on the walls that identified merchants and goods since the populations were mostly illiterate.

For Briciu and Briciu (2016), after the 14th century, with the boost of international commerce, many branding forms were born or developed, and the owners of goods started regularly using certain symbols to differentiate and promote their products. Effectively, at the beginning of the brand concept, brands were used to identify and recognize goods and their manufacturers (Merz et al., 2009), as could have been seen in not only Chinese ceramic goods but also Indian, Greek, and Roman objects. Those had different engravings to identify the property, type, source of the materials, and sometimes the period of its production (Briciu & Briciu, 2016, p.138). Curiously, one English law of 1266 required all bakers to engrave unique symbols on all the loaves they produced and sold to identify those who maliciously tried to sell loaves that weighed less than required by law (Keller, 2003). To Bassat (1999, p.39), "the authentic commercial brand is the result of a historical evolution that has its true origin in the Middle Ages, specifically with the birth of guilds". According to this author, the proliferation of trade guilds used brands to control both the quality and quantity of goods produced. With the growth of cities and the emergence of new social and commercial relationships, the brand guaranteed quality and identified the product, even in the absence of the producer. Although the phenomenon was not transversal or recurrent, except for the tobacco and drug industries, where patents were used, brands were a regional and local phenomenon.

For Aaker (1991), the true pioneering use of the brand was made by the "Old Smuggler" whiskey in 1835 to differentiate itself from imitations and capitalize on its reputation. In fact, at the end of the 19th century, branded products began to gain increasing acceptance in the market. It is precisely here that many brands were born, which remain in the market today, such as Coca-Cola, Philips, Quaker, Cadbury's, Heinz, Peugeot, or AT&T, to name just a few, and the concern with issues of protection and registration of brands arises, with the first specific laws for the defense of trademarks enacted at this time.

It was, therefore, after the industrial revolution that the concept of the brand, as we know it today, gained a great impetus. In the post-industrial revolution, with the development of mechanized production, the relative lack of differentiation between products emerged and the price of products, which were no longer produced manually, dropped drastically, allowing the access of an ever-increasing fringe of the population to more goods, and causing consumption to skyrocket. Even so, the number of industrially produced goods increased so much that even with the rise in consumption, local and regional markets could no longer absorb all this production. Adding to this phenomenon was the advent of the steam engine, the proliferation of railways, and, consequently, the increase in the ease and speed of transport of goods and people, geographically expanding the markets. They went from local to national and from national to international. However, this broke the link between producers and consumers, which in the pre-industrial revolution was close and face-to-face, and artisanal production was based on the laws of supply and demand. In the post-industrial revolution, those who communicated directly with consumers became the large retailers who, receiving products from all cities and countries, concentrated trade and customer relations. The need to attribute to a specific producer the exclusive right to a trademark was, in fact, the first legal framework of the brands, the aim of which was precisely to protect producers and avoid confusion with competing products.

This understanding remained, for decades, as the definition of the main function of the brand, which used to play an essentially differentiating role. Brands emerge, therefore, as a distinctive and identifying sign of the product's origin but simultaneously as a way of enhancing its value to consumers. Its importance was also boosted by this need to communicate with increasingly dispersed and unknown consumers, added by the creation and development of mass media – namely with the technological inventions introduced in the means of printing (appearance of rotating presses) and the cheapening of paper – and the spread of an urban way of life, at the end of the 19th century.

At this stage, and during the early 1900s, brands were, as seen, mere identifiers of the producers of the products. The marketing literature suggests that, on the one hand, companies use brands to show their ownership and take responsibility for the products they produce. On the other hand, brands also help customers to identify and recognize a firm's goods on sight. In spite of the numerous definitions for the concept of the brand, two different points of view can be considered from the outset: that of consumers and that of organizations.

From the consumers' point of view, the brand can be considered the synthesis of real and virtual, objective and subjective experiences lived regarding a product, service, company, institution, or even a person. That is, it is a conglomeration of facts, feelings, attitudes, beliefs, and values that relate to that set of name(s) and symbol(s) directly and regarding both other brands in the same category and to all others that are part of their living universe (Sampaio, 2002). The author adds that the brand acts as an operational facilitator – by simplifying decision processes, as a catalyst – safely accelerating these decision-making processes, and as a form of social expression – by transforming these decisions into facts of social interaction.

From the organizations' perspective, the brand represents a value system and can be considered as the synthesis of the franchise value for the market. To the elements described above regarding how the brand acts, in this case, we can add that the brand also serves as a generator of barriers to entry for existing or potential competitors.

For Merz et al. (2009), the focus of branding between 1900 and 1930 was on individual goods, and the customers remained passive in the brand value creation process while being targeted by the companies.

Meanwhile, the emergence of radio broadcasting in the second decade of the 20th century completely changed the commercial communication of companies and organizations, until then, almost exclusively transmitted through printed media. With the radio, brand communication became more spontaneous and informal, and its widespread acceptance by the population was so great that it became the first truly mass communication medium.

From then until recently, there have been countless forms of commercial denomination and representation, but it seems that the phenomenon only became critical for business and academia in general, from the mid-20th century, with the awareness that brands, effectively, constitute truly important financial assets for their owners.

The academic recognition of brands owes to an article by David Aaker, dating from the early 90s of the last century. Since then, countless studies, analyses, definitions, theories, and methods of evaluating and measuring their impact, value, and influence, both for consumers and for the companies and organizations that own them, have not stopped appearing at a dizzying speed.

In this context, the concept of branding emerges, which can be defined as an intentional strategy that allows the distinction of products in the minds of consumers and guarantees a competitive advantage for companies (Kotler & Keller, 2006; Storie, 2008). Therefore, branding plays a key role in influencing consumers' opinions and preferences about the most varied brands (Bauer et al., 2008). Suppose a brand is a promise of satisfaction (Healey, 2009), a sign, a metaphor acting as an unwritten contract between producer and consumer, seller and buyer, actor and audience, an environment and those who inhabit it, an event and those who experience it. In that case, branding can be understood as the continuous and interactive "management" between producers and their customers in defining that promise and meaning.

More than three decades have elapsed since the publication of the first scientific articles on this topic, and a growing number of authors argue that consumers prefer branded products, make their choices based on brands, are willing to pay more for certain brands, and see them as a contract, a guarantee, deep down as a promise of value and functionality. Nevertheless, we still struggle to define the concept of brand and measure brand equity, determine consumer loyalty, and understand long-term relationships (Ruão, 2006).

In their historical bibliographic review on the development of brands and branding, Merz et al. (2009) identify the second era in its evolution, which dates from 1930 to 1990. For the authors, after the financial crisis resulting from the New York Stock Exchange crash in 1929, branding entered a new phase, with a change in the focus of the interpretation of brands from mere identifiers of products to be seen in terms of image.

With the advent of television (not only appearing in the mid-1930s but only becoming a truly globalized phenomenon after the Second World War), the expansion of the post-war economy, driven largely by social development and economic growth in the US, the generalization of modern commercialization and marketing systems, and, mainly, the expansion of information and communication technologies (ICT), the attention of the main authors focused on the Value of Brands, a consequence of the brand image.

It was believed that images were perceptions created by organizations to enhance their competitive advantages and, therefore, clear and precise communication of the brand image helped consumers distinguish and differentiate each brand from its competition. In addition, several researchers began to study the effects of functional and symbolic benefits of brands and their association with purchase intentions.

Two ways of looking at the brand image emerged: functional images and symbolic images. In the first case, believing that consumers choose brands to satisfy functional, external consumption needs, their function would then consist of creating associations with functional benefits related to consumers' perceptions of how brands satisfy or anticipate their utility needs. In this context, characteristics such as the brand name, for example, stand out as important assets in the consumers' decision-making process. In the second case, with products becoming increasingly similar in their functional utility, consumers began to experience more difficulties distinguishing and differentiating products based solely on their functionality. Thus, from the mid-50s of the last century, some authors began to suggest that brands could gain competitive advantages by also promising symbolic benefits that fulfilled customer's internal needs, such as the possibility of association with one desired group, social role, or self-image, for example (Merz et al., 2009).

According to Castro (2002), David Ogilvy, a well-known advertising expert, brought the task of building the brand image to the center of the commercial communication debate at a meeting of the American Association of Advertising Agencies in 1955. He quoted the article[1] by Gardner and Levy, published shortly before in the Harvard Business Review, arguing that "each advertisement should be seen as an integral part of the long-term investment in the brand personality" and concluded by stating that consumers' choice is determined, often, by the identification with the image projected by the brand of their choice.

It was at that time that one of the most famous and well-known definitions of a brand appeared, by the American Association of Marketing (AMA), in 1960: "(...) a name, term, sign, symbol or design, or a combination thereof, intended to identify the goods and services of one seller or group of sellers and to differentiate them from those of competitors".

This definition mirrors the trend of that time and emphasizes not only the separation but also the superiority of the brand compared to the product. That is, the brand adds intangible characteristics, such as feelings, affections, ideas, and values, which it overvalues regarding the functional performance of the product. The such idea led Keller (2003, p.7) to affirm that it is possible to "(...) make a distinction between the AMA definition of a "brand" with a small b and the industry's concept of a "Brand" with a big B". This perspective became known as the idealistic trend of brands, which considered brand and product as distinct entities. Wolfgang Grassi (1998) argues that idealists see brands as entities that can be manipulated and, therefore, whose attitudes and mental dispositions of consumers towards them would be capable of being shaped by the marketing mix.

> A product is something that is made in a factory; a brand is something that is bought by a customer. A product can be copied by a competitor; a brand is unique. A product can be quickly outdated; a successful brand is timeless.
>
> Stephen King, *in* Seetharaman et al. (2001)

Such as Kotler and Keller (2006) believe the difference between a brand and a commodity lies in the ability of the first to add a set of values and benefits to the basic functionality of a commodity or simple raw material, the defenders of this idealistic trend also believed that brands were theoretical constructions, intangible, manipulable, and the only ones capable of truly transmitting the specificity and uniqueness of the companies' proposal.

From this perspective, in the 1960s, the concept of brand equity was born, which aimed to materialize the accounting of the added value that brands added to (or subtracted from) products. However, it was only in the 1980s that this concept gained momentum both in academia and in the business world. For Aaker (1991, p.15), brand equity can be understood as "a set of assets and liabilities linked to a brand, its name and symbol that add or subtract from the value provided by a product or service to a company and/or to the customers of that company".

From the 1980s onwards, a new trend began to emerge, known as the realistic trend. This perspective continues to consider that brands are specific and intangible attributes that add (or take away) value from products but argues that these need their tangibility to be associated with the products they identify. In other words, this perspective assumes the brand is a holistic entity, made up of tangible and intangible, material and immaterial elements (Ruão, 2006). Randazzo (1996, p.24) agrees, assuming brands as simultaneously physical and perceptual entities. Its material condition is generally static and finite, while the perceptual aspect exists in the psychological space – in the consumer's mind – being, therefore, dynamic and malleable and can be used as a mirror reflecting the current and potential consumer's lifestyle and values. Sampaio (2002) goes even further and defines the brand as a holistic phenomenon, which needs to be analyzed as a whole, given the set of its many parts: product or service formulation; production process; quality; distribution system; communication; sales mechanisms; price; after-sales assistance, and many other factors that interact to make the brand a unique set.

This strand of realistic thought brought, among others, two immediate consequences. Firstly, it allowed an anthropomorphic view of brands, giving them human characteristics such as personality traits, attitudes, and values. Secondly, it brought to the theoretical discussion the new concept of brand identity.

Duarte and Gregório (2022, p.169) stated in their Empathic Brands model, "through the humanization of the brands, consumers proceed understanding them as their partners, originating a closer, deeper, lasting, empathic, social, emotional, and loving relationship". Effectively, the association of human characteristics with brands helps them become active players in the consumer experience, standing out significantly from those who are observed only as objects (Yang et al., 2019).

On the other hand, until now, attention was focused on the Image, that is, on how the public received and interpreted the messages. From now on, attention also focuses on the essence, truth, and coherence of these messages, that is, what the brand is and what it wants to convey: its identity.

With Jean-Nöel Kapferer at the head of this new perspective of brands, with his Brand Identity Prism (2001), identified six facets, namely: physique, personality, relationship, culture, reflection, and self-image, that can be managed by the companies, and on which the brand equity depends.

The physical dimension concerns the objective characteristics present in the consumer's memory that emerge immediately to the mind. Personality, or character, is the set of traits that the consumer associates with human characteristics, and the dimension of Relationship represents the role of the brand in consumers' lives. Culture is the system of values that inspires the brand, Reflection is the projection of the potential buyer or user of the brand, and Self-Image is the dimension that the consumer assumes by associating with the brand.

With this change, branding enters, according to Merz et al. (2009), the third era of its development: the so-called Relationship-focus era, which, according to the authors, took place between 1990 and 2000 and switched from the brand image as the main driver of the brand value to the customer as the principal actor in the brand value creation process. Three main ideas emerged from this era: Brand as Knowledge, Brand as Relationship, and Brand as a Promise.

In the first moment, the authors started to study how customers internalize brand information and how brand value is created. The focus was on the relationship between the customer and the firm, and there was when most brand equity models were created (e.g., Brand Equity Ten from David

Aaker, Customer-Based Brand Equity from Kevin Kane Keller, or the Multidimensional model from Leslie de Chernatony, among others). From this moment forward, the branding literature evolved from viewing the customers as passive in brand value creation to active co-creators.

In the late 1990s and early 2000s, scholars started looking at the role of brands in customers' lives and the relations that customers formed with brands now seen as partners. Researchers found that customers tend to create affect-laden relationships with brands that help them express their personality, self-image, and self-enhancement. That is where the concept of emotional branding emerges, with Berry (2000) advocating that brands should generate emotional value, such as closeness and affection, more than just getting pure economic value. Also, Grönroos's (1994) relationship marketing concept, Jennifer Aaker's (1997) brand personality construct, and Fournier's (1998) brand relationship framework are good examples of this customer-brand relationship focus that sees brands as relationship partners. According to Ruão (2006), it was at the AMA Summer Educator's Conference in 1997 that a call to attention emerged for a new marketing model based on the search for stable and positive forms of interaction and relationship between brands and all their stakeholders, based on the dual dimension: emotional and social. On the emotional side, largely supported by the authors' works above, establishing long-term affective ties and intimacy was defended to stimulate long-term loyalty. In the social dimension, in addition to the shared benefits, brands should also assume a meaning that translates into a "symbolic contract that presupposes the transfer of values, principles, and images" (Ruão, 2006, p.48), with which consumers should identify and use as a form of self-expression. In other words, the success of this relationship marketing depends on the consumers' perception of the brand's attitudes. The connection will be more robust and lasting if consumers feel aligned with those values and attitudes. We will return to this topic at the end of this chapter.

Continuing with the branding evolution literature, the researchers also started looking into the relationship between the firm and the brand itself, analyzing the impact of internal customers (employees) in co-creating the brand value. In this perspective, employees are seen as those who represent the firms' vision and culture, so they are the ones that represent and shape the promises made by the organizations to external customers. Brands were, therefore, seen as promises. Several authors refer that many customer's choices are affected by the assessment they do about the people "behind the product", assuming that employees are an important asset that may help the companies achieve their goals and create or maintain their competitive advantage and a fundamental component in the brand value creation (King, 1991). Berry (2000) also highlights the employees' critical importance in brand building, assuming they play a greater role than the product itself.

Finally, the last branding era, which started in the early 2000s and is still ongoing, is known as the stakeholder-focus brand era. At the beginning of this century, the "logic of a brand started to shift from a firm-provided property of goods to a brand as collaborative, value co-creation activity of firms and all their stakeholders" (Merz et al., 2009, p.328–329). In this era, brands are viewed as continuous social processes, where their value is permanently constructed through dynamic social interactions among all the stakeholders. These social interactions between groups of people sharing the same interest and admiration for a specific brand gave birth to the brand communities. These communities are highly loyal, true believers, and the strongest advocates of the brands, even if some may not even own the brand. Although they are not the only group that influences and affects brand value creation, they are a very important part of the process. This stakeholder perspective is supported by the writings of the Marketing Guru Seth Godin (2019, p.17), "Effective marketing is now based on empathy and service, instead of selfish mass strategies", highlighting exactly that is the process, not the output that really matters in terms of brand value creation.

In sum, the literature evolved from viewing brand value as determined through value-in-exchange to a new perspective that sees the brand value as a perceived value-in-use by the set of all the stakeholders. Customers, employees, admirers, and all the other ones that, for some reason, impact or are impacted by the brand. That is precisely where the "new consumer", more active, more informed, more socially concerned, more environmentally responsible, and more politically and ethically aware, enters the equation.

1.2   The new consumer

"Consumer is god" is now the new mantra for businesses and organizations worldwide. This idea came from a sentence by Michael Dell, Founder of Dell Computers, based on the perspective that the consumer should be effectively treated as the god of the entire market, which should not be contested, even when he is wrong (Sampaio, 2002). In fact, the consumer has the power to decide whether to buy, when, and what and thus decide which brands and companies survive. On top of this idea, Regis McKenna (1997) added an another relevant concept: the consumer is never satisfied. Consequently, companies and organizations must permanently listen to and perceive their anxieties, desires, needs, values, and expectations to anticipate them, proposing changes even before they realize that the existing products and services no longer serve their wishes adequately. That may be the rule number one to survive and prosper in today's market. As rule number two, brands must incorporate each era's trends and the socio-cultural changes of their audiences, with whom they must maintain a dialogue (Perez, 2004, p.14). Without this and a permanent interaction: listen, act, listen, react, the brands may lose its attractiveness and thus become worn out, degraded, and even disappear.

At the beginning of the 21st century, we are less and less "citizens of the world" and more and more "consumers of a global market" (Lewis & Bridges, 2004). Effectively, consumerism or *hyperconsumerism*, as Lipovetsky and Serroy (2010) called it, is probably the most striking feature of current times. The big difference between actual consumers and those who preceded us is not the chronological age but attitudes and behaviors towards consumption, with brands revealing themselves as the great icons of the 20th century and invading the 21st century with all their intensity and presence (Perez, 2004, p.4).

The literature on brands is vast and diverse, offering numerous perspectives on them, their scope, purpose, value, etc. In the context of this book, we will understand them as systems of meaning: the way all their stakeholders understood them. In a bewildering world of competitive clamor, in which rational choice has become almost impossible, brands represent clarity, trust, consistency, status, and especially belonging – everything that allows human beings to define themselves. Brands represent identity (Olins, 2003) and assume prominence in buying and selling relationships, going beyond the idea of mere facilitators of commercial transactions to transform themselves into powerful and complex signs of social positioning in the world (Perez, 2004, p.3).

When we search for the origin of the word "consume", we realize that it comes directly from the Latin *consumere*, which means "to use up, eat, waste". According to the online etymology dictionary[2] from the late XIV century, "to consume" means "to destroy by separating into parts which cannot be reunited, as by burning or eating", hence "destroy the substance of, annihilate". Curiously, instead of destroying something, consumption creates jobs, stimulates the economy, and boosts taxes; in short, it is inseparable from today's society.

The new consumers are independent, individualistic, involved, and knowledgeable about the products. Unlike their predecessors, who were constrained by a lack of money, options, and availability of the products, new consumers face a lack of time, attention, and confidence (Lewis & Bridges, 2004).

With the old theory of the "homo economicus" – based on the assumption that agents act strictly following the scheme of individualistic rational optimization (Urbina & Ruiz-Villaverde, 2019) – already disused, the new consumers use the consumption act as a way of expressing their individuality and even their most personal values, as environmental concerns, social issues, or political intentions, among others. This new behavior is known as "political consumerism".

1.3   Social and political consumerism

According to Kapferer (2008, p.22), brands have eight functions: (1) *Identification*, to be clearly seen, to identify the sought-after products quickly, and to structure the shelf perception. (2) *Practicality*, to allow time and energy savings through identical repurchasing and loyalty. (3) *Guarantee*, to be sure of finding the same quality no matter where or when you buy the product or service. (4) *Optimization*, to be sure of buying the best product in its category, the best performer for a particular purpose. (5) *Badge*, to have confirmation of your self-image or the image you present to others. (6) *Continuity*, satisfaction created by a relationship of familiarity and intimacy with the brand consumers have been consuming for years. (7) *Hedonistic*, enchantment linked to the attractiveness of the brand, its logo, its communication, and its experiential rewards. And (8) *Ethical*, satisfaction linked to the responsible behavior of the brand in its relationship with society (ecology, employment, citizenship, and advertising which does not shock).

Effectively, brands can no longer dissociate themselves from the moral and ethical concerns of consumers who increasingly demand corporate responsibility from organizations. In fact, organizations will be better positioned if their branding practices reflect the cultural and ideological trends of the whole society (Merz et al., 2009).

We are living in a new relationship model in which consumers, once passive, now demand an active posture and attitude in the involvement and fulfillment of social, community, and planetary causes from companies and brands. As Cornelissen (2014, p.359) states, there has been a shift in the traditional conception of the company as an entity whose sole maxim is the creation of monetary value – profit – and the commitment and satisfaction of shareholders, towards an organization with several responsibilities to the society, with an emphasis on the communities it affects. In other words, the social issues that affect and mobilize populations also concern companies that intend to establish and maintain relationships with them in a balanced symbiosis between the objectives of communities and corporations. Today, the consumer not only praises but also criticizes, listens, speaks, acts, interacts, analyzes, and opinionates (Duarte & Freitas, 2021).

In addition to expectations regarding corporate citizenship, there is another main reason for brands' social concern: political consumerism (Clarke, 2008; Stolle & Micheletti, 2013; van Deth, 2014). "Political consumerism" can be defined from the specific involvements [of the consumer] in the market, a consequence of social concerns associated with consumption and production (Boström et al., 2019). It can involve religious, ethnic, family issues, gender, environmental, and animal rights themes, to mention a few. Now, this reality cannot just be seen as a tendency of an activist minority. Studies such as those by Stolle and Micheletti (2005) conclude that the use of *buycotting* and *boycotting* – actions with political significance – has been increasing among consumers, indicating that more and more consumers evaluate the moral and ethical image they have of a certain brand, product, or company in their purchasing process. In the USC report (2022, p.15), 85% of professionals responsible for communication believe that the number of companies that defend a cause will increase in the next five years, and 73% say that their own companies and clients will increase their public engagement already this year.

In this context of intense scrutiny, the society is subject to by the public sphere – namely in social networks, not only by activists, groups, and organizations but also by the media – brands, currently placed in the sphere of public debate, increasingly need to dialogue with all their stakeholders actively. Moreover, they must also identify and associate themselves with causes and social movements to assume their own "social positioning".

As Duarte and Freitas (2021, p.1) stated,

> In a world where every consumer has an opinion, the power of brands is increasingly entrenched between the values it defends and the attitudes it practices, and, on the other hand, the image and opinion it transmits and the way they are perceived. In this context, the "social brands" construct emerged.

Notes

1 Gardner, B. & Levy, S. (1955). "The Product and the Brand," *Harvard Business Review*, March-April, 33–39.
2 https://www.etymonline.com/word/consume.

References

Aaker, D. A. (1991). *Managing brand equity: Capitalizing on the value of a brand name*. New York: The Free Press.

Aaker, J. L. (1997). Dimensions of brand personality. *Journal of Marketing Research, 34*(3), 347–356.

Bassat, L. (1999). *El libro rojo de las marcas. Como construir marcas de êxito*. Madrid: Espasa Calpe.

Bauer, H. H., Stokburger-Sauer, N. E., & Exler, S. (2008). Brand image and fan loyalty in professional team sport: A refined model and empirical assessment. *Journal of Sport Management, 22*(2), 205–226. https://doi.org/10.1123/jsm.22.2.205

Berry, L. (2000). Cultivating service brand equity. *Journal of the Academy of Marketing Science, 28*(1), 128–137.

Boström, M., Micheletti, M., & Oosterveer, P. (2019). *The Oxford handbook of political consumerism*. New York: Oxford University Press.

Briciu, V. A., & Briciu, A. (2016). A brief history of brands and the evolution of place branding. *Bulletin of the Transilvania University of Brasov, 9*(58), 137–142.

Castro, J. (2002). *Comunicação de marketing*. Lisboa: Ed. Sílabo.

Clarke, N. (2008). From ethical consumerism to political consumption. *Geography Compass, 2*(6), 1870–1884. https://doi.org/10.1111/j.1749-8198.2008.00170.x

Cornelissen, J. (2014). *Corporate communication: A guide to theory and practice -4th Edition*. Dorchester: SAGE.

Duarte, A., & Freitas, J. (2021). Social brands: The future of branding? *Academia Letters*, Article 455. https://doi.org/10.20935/AL455

Duarte, A., & Gregório, M. (2022). Empathic brands: Proposing a model for its measure and evaluation. In Andrade, J. G. & Ruão, T. (Eds.), *Navigating digital communication and challenges for organizations* (pp. 168–185). IGI Global. https://doi.org/10.4018/978-1-7998-9790-3.ch010

Fournier, S. (1998). Consumers and their brands: Developing relationship theory in consumer research. *Journal of Consumer Research, 24*(4), 343–373.

Gardner, B., & Levy, S. (1955). "The product and the brand," *Harvard Business Review*, March–April, 33–39.

Global Communication Report. (2022). *The future of Corporate Activism*, USC Annenberg School for Communication and Journalism, Acedido a 7 de setembro de 2022 em. https://annenberg.usc.edu/research/center-public-relations/global-communication-report

Godin, S. (2019). *Isto é marketing [This is marketing]*. Porto: Ideias de Ler.

Grassi, W. (1998). The reality of brands: Towards an ontology of marketing. *American Journal of Economics and Sociology, 58*(2), 313–359.

Grönroos, C. (1994). From marketing mix to relationship marketing: Towards a paradigm shift in marketing. *Management Decision, 32*(2), 4–20.

Healey, M. (2009). *O que é o branding?* Barcelona: Gustavo Gili.

Kapferer, J.-N. (2001). *Reinventing the brand*. London: Kogan Page.

Kapferer, J.-N. (2008). *The new strategic brand management: Creating and sustaining brand equity long term*. London and Sterling, VA: Kogan Page Publishers.

Keller, K. L. (2003). Understanding brands, branding and brand equity. *Interactive Marketing, 5*(1), 7–20.

Khan, S., & Mufti, O. (2007). The hot history & cold future of brands. *Journal of Managerial Sciences, 1*(1), 75–87.

King, S. (1991). Brand-building in the 1990s. *Journal of Marketing Management, 7*(1), 3–13. https://doi.org/10.1080/0267257X.1991.9964136

Kotler, P., & Keller, K. L. (2006). *Marketing para o século XXI*. Pearson: Prentice Hall.

Lee, S., & Heere, B. (2018). Exploring the relative effectiveness of emotional, rational, and combination advertising appeals on sport consumer behavior. *Sport Marketing Quarterly, 27*(2), 82–92.

Lewis, D., & Bridges, D. (2004). *A Alma do novo consumidor*. São Paulo: M Books do Brasil

Lipovetsky, G., & Serroy, J. (2010). *A Cultura-Mundo. Resposta a uma sociedade desorientada*. Lisboa: Edições 70.

McKenna, R. (1997). *Real time: Preparing for the age of the never satisfied customer*. Boston, MA: Harvard Business Press.

Merz, M. A., He, Y., & Vargo, S. L. (2009). The evolving brand logic: A service-dominant logic perspective. *Journal of the Academy of Marketing Science, 37*(3), 328–344.

Olins, W. (2003). *A marca*. Lisboa: Editorial Verbo.

Perez, C. (2004). *Signos da marca: Expressividade e Sensorialidade*. São Paulo: Pioneira Thomson Learning.

Rajaram, S., & Shelly, C. S. (2012). History of branding. *International Journal of Social Sciences & Interdisciplinary Research, 1*(3), 100–104.

Randazzo, S. (1996). *A criação de mitos na publicidade: Como os publicitários usam o poder do mito e do simbolismo para criar marcas de sucesso*. Rio de Janeiro: Rocco.

Ruão, T. (2006). *Marcas e identidades: Guia da concepção e gestão das marcas comerciais*. Porto: Campo das Letras.

Sampaio, R. (2002). *Marcas de A a Z. Como construir e manter marcas de sucesso.* Rio de Janeiro: Campus.

Seetharaman, A., Nazdir, M., & Gunalan, S. (2001). A conceptual study on brand valuation. *Journal of Product & Brand Management, 10*(4), 243–256.

Stolle, D., Hooghe, M., & Micheletti, M. (2005). Politics in the supermarket: Political consumerism as a form of political participation. *International Political Science Review, 26*(3), pp. 245–269. https://doi.org/10.1177/0192512105053784

Stolle, D., & Micheletti, M. (2013). *Political consumerism: Global responsibility in action.* Cambridge: Cambridge University Press.

Storie, J. (2008). Professional athletes, sports: The ultimate branding. *Fort Worth Business Press, 22*(26), 13.

Urbina, D. A., & Ruiz-Villaverde, A. (2019). A critical review of homo economicus from five approaches. *American Journal of Economics and Sociology, 78*(1), 63–93.

USC Annenberg Center for Public Relations. (2022). *The future of Corporate Activism,* Global Communication Report, Acedido a 14 de Setembro de 2022. https://annenberg.usc.edu/research/center-public-relations/global-communication-report

van Deth, J. W. (2014). A conceptual map of political participation. *Acta Política, 49*(3), 349–367. https://doi.org/10.1057/ap.2014.6

World Business Council for Sustainable Development (WBCSD). (2000). *Corporate social responsibility: Making good business sense.* Geneva: World Business Council for Sustainable Development.

Yang, L. W., Aggarwal, P., & McGill, A. L. (2019). The 3 C's of anthropomorphism: Connection, comprehension, and competition. *Counselling Psychology Review, 3*(1), 3–19.

2 Institutional brand communication management in pandemic times

The engagement of publics

José Gabriel Andrade

CECS / Universidade do Minho

We begin this chapter with a review focuses on the publics and new publics that crisis periods can present. It has observed the level of participation in face of the problems and crisis.

In the second part, we will look at the pandemic crisis caused by Covid-19, discussing the impact on brands and analyzing the communication of institutional brands in Portugal during the time of crisis.

Finally, we analyze the case study of the University of Minho in crisis communication during the pandemic time, believing it to be a social brand concept.

2.1 The relationship of the public with the institutional brands

Strategic communication publics have been guided by a core of central questions that Botan and Soto (1998) identify as (a) definition, what are the publics; (b) segmentation, how to significantly differentiate publics; (c) function, what roles different publics play in society; and (d) process, how publics come into existence and respond in a certain way. These issues have been addressed by authors from different perspectives with evident hegemony of the situational perspective introduced by Grunig and Repper (1992). According to this point of view, a public is considered to result from a state motivated by a problematic situation and does not constitute a permanent state of consciousness. It is believed that publics appear as responses to problematic situations and that they self-organize to solve them. This perspective considers the segmentation of publics through certain variables. The variables pointed out by Grunig and Repper (1992) are inferred (cognitions, attitudes, and perceptions) and objectivized (demographics, media usage patterns, and geographic location). The construction of this model is associated with most studies in marketing, advertising and public relations.

The situational theory of publics by Grunig and Repper (1992) is part of a broader context, seeking to defend a strategic management model for strategic communication. The main concern was to build a reference framework to

DOI: 10.4324/9781003382331-3

explain the evolution of the behavior of certain social groups towards a given organization. Three states of development of these groups were defined: the stakeholder state, the public state, and the subject state. Stakeholders are understood as those who affect an organization with their decisions or are affected by the organization's decisions. When stakeholders recognize a problem, they increase their level of involvement, and if they are willing to get involved to address that problem, they move to a state of publics and may stay there for a longer or shorter time. Finally, if the publics are not satisfied with the behavior of a particular organization, one may reach the state of issues or controversies (Eiró-Gomes & Duarte, 2005). The situational variables that are involved in the shift from stakeholders to publics include (a) problem recognition, which leads to information seeking, (b) constraint recognition, which discourages communication since people do not communicate about issues, they feel they cannot do anything about, and (c) level of involvement, as an individual's cognitive perception of his or her connection to a given situation. An audience is more likely to be active when its constituents perceive that what an organization does involve them (Level of Involvement), that the consequences of what an organization does constitute a problem (Problem Recognition), and that they will not be embarrassed if they do something about the problem (Constraint Recognition) (Eiró-Gomes & Duarte, 2005).

With the advance of information and communication technologies and observing the transformation of the publics, it makes sense to report to the communication strategy the proposal of Sonia Livingstone (2005), who presents the notion of audiences and publics not as opposite contexts, although they are different notions, with many similarities. For the author, "the analysis of publics focuses on an attempt to understand the meaning and consequences of public, as opposed to private, forms of activity or spaces for that activity" (Livingstone, 2005, p.35). According to Livingstone, media (traditional and new media) provide a window into the world (Livingstone, 2005, p.21) to mediatize, select, assign priorities, shape, according to the institutions, information and communication technologies, and discursive conventions of the media industry. Sonia Livingstone refers to civic citizenship (Livingstone, 2005, p.34) to speak of a withdrawn public, from privacy, that can generate social capital to achieve greater engagement, with forms of identity.

At the organizational level, crisis and risk management requires special attention to the public, both internally and externally. Therefore, in terms of communication, it is convenient for the manager to define priority groups for informative action. However, with the development of the new media and the internet and the increasing movement of people, the management of information flows can no longer be viewed only locally or regionally. The globalization of markets and societies in general suggests considering audiences on a more global level, including both actual and potential audiences.

To encourage investment in small businesses and prevent abuses by businesses and investors, the regulation requires that to be eligible for the EIS scheme, the company (or the group of companies of which it is the parent company) must meet the following conditions at the time the shares are issued:

- be permanently established in the United Kingdom;
- not be listed on a recognised stock exchange;
- not control another company other than qualifying subsidiaries;
- not be controlled by another company, or do not have more than 50% of their shares owned by another company;
- do not expect to close after completing the project;
- have less than £15 million in gross assets before any shares are issued, and not more than £16 million immediately afterwards;
- have less than 250 full-time employees.

The last two points apply not only to the company but also to any qualifying subsidiaries.

The money raised by the new share issue must be used to grow or develop the company's business and to carry out a qualifying trade within two years of the investment or to conduct research and development activities leading to a qualifying trade. The raised money cannot be used for the total or partial acquisition of another company. The shares issued for EIS investments must be full-risk, non-redeemable ordinary shares with no special rights over the company's assets. These shares can have limited preferential rights to dividends which, however, are neither cumulative nor variable.

To avoid the definition of agreements made with the sole purpose of taking advantage of the tax benefits provided by the EIS, the regulation establishes that:

- investors must hold the shares for at least three years;
- investors must pay for shares as they receive them;
- reciprocity agreements in which the company invests back in an investor's company in exchange for its investment are not permitted;
- the investment cannot be guaranteed against risks.

The EIS grants investors tax relief of 30% on investments of up to £1 million per tax year (or up to £2 million if the money is invested in knowledge-intensive companies). This means that 30% of what the investor pays for the shares turns into a tax credit which reduces the investor's individual income tax owed for the year. In addition to the tax credit, the EIS offers investors tax-free capital gains if the shares in an EIS-eligible company are held for at least three years (from either the date of issue or the commencement of trading, whichever is later). This means that no Capital Gains Tax (CGT) is payable on any profits at the point of disposal. Investors can hold the shares for longer than the three-year qualifying period. In this case, if the company continues to grow, the CGT-free gains will accrue over a longer period and will be exempt from CGT. The EIS also provides investors with the possibility to defer up to 50% of the tax liability of a capital gain (arising from the sale of any other asset) by investing that gain into an EIS-eligible opportunity. Loss relief can be claimed against both income tax and capital gains tax if an unexpected event arises with the portfolio company which results in the investor's EIS shares being disposed of at a loss (if the shares have been held for at least three years).

Different rules are established for knowledge-intensive companies, which carry out a significant amount of research, development, or innovation at the time the shares are issued. To qualify as a knowledge-intensive company, the company and any qualifying subsidiaries must have at the time the shares are issued: (i) less than 500 full-time employees; (ii) 20% of employees with masters or higher degrees carrying out research for at least three years from the date of investment; and (iii) work to create intellectual property and expect the majority of the business to come from it within ten years. These companies can raise up to £10 millions of investment per year and £20 millions of investment in their lifetime (including the amounts received from other venture capital schemes). To apply as a knowledge-intensive company, it must have been less than ten years since the company's first commercial sale or from the time when its annual turnover went over £200,000. In addition, the regulation requires knowledge-intensive companies to invest 10% a year for three years or 15% in one of three years of their overall operating costs on research, development, or innovation. If the company is at least three years old, it must have invested this amount in the three years before the investment. If the company is less than three years old, it must do this in the three years following the investment. Investors are allowed to invest up to £2 million, if at least £1 millions of this is intended for knowledge-intensive companies.

The Seed Enterprise Investment Scheme (SEIS) was launched in 2012 to stimulate investment in qualifying new seed-stage companies. It provides individuals with income tax relief on 50% of the value of the investment, with a maximum of £200,00 of the investments per tax year (£100,000 a year before April 2023). Investors can claim income tax relief in the tax year they invest in or the year before. In addition to this, investors can also benefit from up to 50% Capital Gains Tax relief (up to a maximum of £50,000) on gains that are reinvested in EIS-eligible shares in the same tax year. Any gain arising on the disposal of the shares may also be exempt from Capital Gains Tax if the shares are held for a minimum of three years. Loss relief can be claimed against any of the investor's taxable earnings if the investor suffers a loss on the disposal of SEIS shares at any time.

To be eligible for the SEIS scheme, the company must meet the following conditions at the time the shares are issued:

- be established in the United Kingdom;
- carry out a new qualifying trade;
- not be listed on the stock exchange, and do not have (with their subsidiaries) an arrangement to become listed;
- not control another company other than qualifying subsidiaries;
- not be controlled by another company since the incorporation date of the company;
- not have (including any of its subsidiaries) gross assets over £200,000 and more than 25 full-time employees;
- been trading for no more than two years;
- not be (including any of its subsidiaries) a member of a partnership;
- not have received investment through the Enterprise Investment Scheme (EIS) or from a venture capital trust (VCT).

The companies that comply with the above requirements can receive a maximum of £150,000 through SEIS per year, including any other state aid received in the three years up to the date of the investment. Investors will lose the tax reliefs offered by the SEIS if the company fails to comply with the rules for at least three years after the investment is made. The money raised by the new share issue must be spent within three years of the issue on a qualifying trade or on research and development activities that will lead to a qualifying trade. The money cannot be used to buy shares unless these are in a qualifying 90% subsidiary that uses the money for a qualifying business activity. As for the EIS, also for the SEIS the regulation requires that the shares are paid up in full, in cash, when they are issued. In addition, shares must be full-risk, non-redeemable ordinary shares with no special rights over the company's assets. These shares can have limited preferential rights to dividends which, however, are neither cumulative nor variable. Arrangements of any kind to raise funds for the purpose of tax evasion or for the sole purpose of obtaining tax relief are not permitted.

2.5.4 *Belgium*

To support the creation of start-ups and the growth of start-ups (i.e., scale-ups), SMEs, and micro-enterprises, the Belgian government adopted the 'Start-up Plan'. Launched in 2015, this legal framework includes a tax incentive scheme, called 'the Tax Shelter for start-ups', available for both direct investments and investments via crowdfunding platforms recognised by the Authority for Financial Services and Markets (FSMA). This tax incentive scheme allows natural persons subject to personal income tax or non-resident tax in Belgium to deduct, respectively, 25%, 30%, or 45% of their investment in shares of scale-ups, SMEs (or start-ups), and micro-enterprises (or early-stage start-ups) from the taxes due on their revenue up to €100,000 per taxable period and per taxpayer. To qualify for the tax reduction under the Tax Shelter, the investor must hold the shares for at least four years and cannot hold more than 30% of the company's shares. The investment cannot be in a company that focuses on management, real estate, or investment. Legal entities (i.e., non-profits, companies, and cooperatives) cannot benefit from the Tax Shelter.

Scale-ups are companies aged between five and ten years at the date of the investment which, in the two previous financial years, have achieved an annual growth of at least 10% in employment and/or turnover. Investment in these companies benefit from a tax reduction of 25% as they are less risky than micro-enterprises. To qualify for the Tax Shelter, scale-ups must not exceed more than one of the following limits:

- have a turnover of less than €9,000,000;
- have less than 50 full-time employees;
- have a total balance sheet of less than €4,500,000.

The scale-ups that comply with the above requirements can receive a maximum of €1,000,000 through Tax Shelter per year.

Small and medium enterprises (SMEs) or start-ups are companies less than four years old that do not exceed more than one of the following limits:

- have a turnover of less than €7,300,000;
- have less than 50 full-time employees (or less than 100 employees if other limits are met);
- have a total balance sheet of less than €3,650,000.

SMEs that comply with the above requirements can receive a maximum of €500,000 through Tax Shelter per year. Investments in these companies are granted a 30% tax reduction.

Finally, micro-enterprises or early-stage start-ups are companies less than four years old that do not exceed more than one of the following limits:

- have a turnover of less than €700,000;
- have less than ten full-time employees;
- have a total balance sheet of less than €350,000.

Micro-enterprises that comply with the above requirements can receive a maximum of €500,000 through Tax Shelter per year. Investments in these companies receive a higher tax reduction of 45% as they are considered riskier than investments in SMEs and scale-ups.

To be eligible for the Tax Shelter, the company must meet the following conditions at the time the shares are issued:

- be registered in Belgium;
- not be listed and have not previously distributed dividends or made a capital reduction;
- not be the result of a merger or a corporate spin-off operation;
- not be involved in an insolvency process;
- have not previously raised €500,000 (for start-ups) or €1,000,000 (for scale-ups) in funds under the Tax Shelter;
- carry out the capital increase (seed or series funding) under the Tax Shelter law within the first four years of their incorporation (for start-ups) or within the fifth and tenth years of their incorporation (for scale-ups);
- not transform during the four-year Tax Shelter period its business into: (i) a management company; (ii) an investment, treasury, or financing company; or (iii) a real estate business (construction, acquisition, management, development, sale, rental, etc.).

Companies cannot use the money raised by the new share for the distribution of dividends, acquisition of shares, or the granting of loans during 48 months from the issue date. The tax reduction must be confirmed each year for four years.

2.5.5 Italy

In Italy, investments in the share capital of innovative start-ups and SMEs registered in the appropriate section of the Italian Business Register benefit from the tax incentives provided for by Article 29 of Law Decree no. 179 of 18 October 2012. These benefits have recently been extended to equity crowdfunding by the Budget Law which came into force on 1 January 2018. The ministerial decree of 7 May 2019 establishes the procedures for implementing the tax incentives for investment in innovative start-ups and innovative SMEs and identifies the companies that fall within the scope of the tax relief. According to Italian law, innovative start-ups are companies based in Italy or in a EU country or in a country adhering to the Agreement on the European Economic Area with a production site or a branch in Italy. Innovative start-ups must meet the following requirements:

- not be listed on a regulated market or on a multilateral trading facility (MTF);
- be incorporated and have been carrying out business activities for no more than 48 months;

- have the principal place of business and interests in Italy;
- not distribute, and have not distributed, profits;
- have the development, production, and marketing of innovative products or services with high technological value as their exclusive or prevalent corporate purpose;
- not have been established by a merger, split-ups, or as a result of the sale of a company or business unit;
- not have, starting from the second year of activity, a total annual production value exceeding five million euro;
- meet at least one of the following additional requirements: (i) a volume of research and development expenditure equal to or greater than 15% of the higher between the cost and the total value of production; (ii) at least one-third of the total workforce must be represented by employees who have a research doctorate (Ph.D.) title or who are carrying out a research doctorate at an Italian or foreign university, or who have a degree and who have carried out, for at least three years, certified research activity at public or private research institutes, in Italy or abroad; (iii) be the owner or depositary or licensee of at least one industrial property right relating to an industrial, biotechnological invention, a semiconductor product topography or a new plant variety directly relating to the corporate object and the activity of the business.

Innovative SMEs are SMEs, as defined by the recommendation of the Commission of the European Communities of 6 May 2003 concerning the definition of micro, small, and medium-sized enterprises (2003/361/EC), which meet the following requirements:

- be stablished in Italy or in a EU country or in a country adhering to the Agreement on the European Economic Area, as long as they have a production site or a branch in Italy;
- not be listed on a regulated market or on a multilateral trading facility (MTF);
- have the latest financial statement and any consolidated financial statements audited by an auditor or an auditing company entered in the register of auditors;
- meet at least two of the following requirements: (i) a volume of research and development expenditure equal to or greater than 3% of the higher between the cost and the total value of production; (ii) at least one-fifth of the total workforce must be represented by employees who have a research doctorate (Ph.D.) title or who are carrying out a research doctorate at an Italian or foreign university, or who have a degree and who have carried out, for at least three years, certified research activity at public or private research institutes, in Italy or abroad; (iii) be the owner or depositary or licensee of at least one

industrial property right relating to an industrial, biotechnological invention, a semiconductor product topography or a new plant variety directly relating to the corporate object and the activity of the business.

To be eligible for the tax benefits, the innovative SMEs must receive the investment before their first commercial sale on a market or within seven years of their first commercial sale. Innovative SMEs' eligibility for tax incentives can be extended from seven to ten years if they certify through an external expert assessment that they have not yet reached their maximum potential to generate returns. The seven-year limit from the first commercial sale does not apply if the innovative SME makes a risk capital investment on the basis of a business plan relating to a new product or a new geographic market which is more than 50% of the average annual turnover of the previous five years.

The Italian tax incentive scheme allows natural persons subject to personal income tax (imposta sul reddito delle persone fisiche – IRPEF) to deduct 30% of their investment in the capital of innovative start-ups and SMEs from the taxes due on their revenue up to €1,000,000 per taxable period and per taxpayer. To qualify for the tax deduction, the investor must hold the investment for at least three years. Legal entities subject to the corporate income tax (imposta sui redditi delle società – IRES) can deduct 30% of their investment in the capital of innovative start-ups and SMEs from their total taxable income up to €1,800,000 per taxable period, as long as the investment is held for at least three years. Investors can carry forward unused tax deductions to the next tax year, but not later than the third. The tax deduction does not apply to investments made through collective investment undertakings and companies, directly or indirectly, with public participation.

Innovative start-ups and SMEs are not eligible for tax benefits in the following cases:

* they operate in the shipbuilding and coal and steel sectors;
* have received unlawful state aid that has not been fully recovered;
* are in a situation of difficulty as defined by the European Commission's Guidelines on State aid for rescuing and restructuring non-financial firms in difficulty (2014/C 249/01).

2.6 Key players in the European equity crowdfunding market

The European equity crowdfunding market has experienced significant growth in recent years, grew from $63.1 million in 2013 to $280 million in 2020 (excluding the United Kingdom) (Ziegler *et al.*, 2021). It contributed 65% to total SME funding ($1.73 billion). In 2020, the United Kingdom has significantly outperformed other European

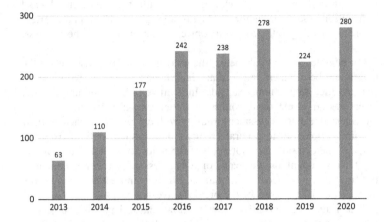

Figure 2.1 Equity-based crowdfunding transaction value in Europe (excluding the United Kingdom) from 2013 to 2020 (USD, millions).

Source: Author's elaboration on data from Ziegler *et al.* (2021).

countries with a market volume of $656 million, followed by France ($432 million), Germany ($375 million), and Italy ($74 million). Figure 2.1 shows the equity-based crowdfunding transaction value in Europe (excluding the United Kingdom) from 2013 to 2020.

The following subparagraphs report a list of the key players in the equity crowdfunding market within four representative countries in Europe (i.e., France, Spain, Italy, and the United Kingdom). These countries were selected based on data availability and the fact that they all have a relatively large equity crowdfunding market volume compared to other European countries and a much more mature crowdfunding ecosystem. Germany was excluded as the websites of the platforms are in German, and therefore it was not possible to collect information on the general conditions of the loans.

2.6.1 *France*

In France, equity-based platforms must be listed in the official register of the French association ORIAS (Registre Unique des Intermédiaires en Assurance Banque et Finance) as a participatory investment advisor (Conseiller en Investissement Participatif – CIP). Alternatively, equity crowdfunding platforms can choose to operate with the status of investment service provider (Prestataire de Services d'Investissement – PSI). In the latter case, the platforms must be enrolled in the Register of Financial Agents (Regafi). The new European crowdfunding regime

(Regulation (EU) 2020/1503) abolished the CIP and PSI status and introduced the new status of 'crowdfunding service provider' (Prestataire de Services de Financement Participatif – PSFP). The PSFP status is mandatory to offer crowdfunding investments throughout the EU as long as the crowdfunding offer is related to commercial activities and does not exceed, over a 12-month period, €5 million per project. The register of authorised crowdfunding service providers is available on the European Securities and Markets Authority (ESMA) website. Table 2.2 shows the list of all equity-based platforms authorised by French law and listed in the ORIAS and Regafi registers.

2.6.2 Spain

To operate, equity crowdfunding platforms must be authorised and registered in the appropriate register held by the Spanish Securities Market Commission (Comisión Nacional del Mercado de Valores – CNMV). The register is published on the CNMV's website and updated regularly. Pursuant to Article 54 of Law 5/2015, it must contain a set of updated information on the platform such as the company name, the website, and the registered office, as well as the identity of the managers and shareholders with significant participation.

To be enrolled on the CNMV register, equity crowdfunding platforms must meet the following requirements (see Article 55 of Law 5/2015): (i) have the exclusive corporate purpose of carrying out activities reserved for crowdfunding platforms (i.e., putting investors in contact, professionally and via a website, with the promoters of the campaigns); (ii) have a legal and administrative headquarters in Spain or in another member state of the EU; (iii) be established as joint stock companies only; (iv) platform directors must meet the requirements of reputation, knowledge, and experience necessary to perform their duties; (v) have a good administrative and accounting organisation or adequate internal audit procedures; (vi) have suitable means to guarantee the security, confidentiality, reliability, and capacity of the services provided by electronic means; (vii) have an internal code of conduct that considers possible conflicts of interest; and (viii) have adequate means to ensure that in the event of cessation of its activity, the platform can continue to provide all or part of the services it had committed to for projects that have obtained funding. Law 5/2015 also requires equity crowdfunding platforms to meet certain financial requirements (see Article 56) such as a fully paid-up share capital of at least €60.000, or a professional indemnity insurance, surety, or other equivalent guarantee with a minimum cover of €300.000 per claim and a total of €400.000 per year for all claims, or a combination of share capital and professional indemnity insurance, surety, or other equivalent security giving rise to

Table 2.2 List of French equity crowdfunding platforms

Platform	Foundation year	City	Website	Industry focus
1001pact (LITA.co)	2015	Paris	fr.lita.co	General
Ab funding	2014	Lyon	ab-funding.com	General
Anaxago	2012	Paris	anaxago.com	General
Booster health	2014	Creteil	boosterhealth.com	Healthcare, Biotech, MedTech
Bulb in town	2012	Paris	bulbintown.com	General
Enerfip	2014	Montpellier	fr.enerfip.eu	Renewable energy
Finple	2015	Vertou	finple.com	Start-up and real estate
Feedelios	2013	Ponte-a-pitre	feedelios.com	General
Greenchannel	2015	Nanterre	greenchannel.fr	Energetic transition
GwenneG	2015	Rennes	gwenneg.bzh/fr	General
Happy Capital	2013	Paris	happy-capital.com	General
Hoolders	2014	Nanterre	hoolders.com	General
Investbook	2014	Paris	investbook.fr	General
My new startup	2013	Nantes	mynewstartup.com	General
Proximea	2015	Saint-Herblain	proximea.com	Start-up, Real estate, Energy
Sora finance	2014	Paris	sora-finance.com	General
Soul Invest	n/a	Rennes	Soulinvest.com	Impact Investing, Environment
Sowefound	2013	Paris	sowefound.com	Impact Investing
We share bonds	2015	Paris	wesharebonds.com	General
weeXimmo	2014	Paris	weeximmo.com	General
Wine Funding SAS	2014	Bordeaux	winefunding.com	Wine
Wiseed SA	2008	Toulouse	wiseed.com	General

Source: Author's elaboration on data from the ORIAS and Regafi official websites.

a level of cover equal to that set out above. The Securities Market Commission supervises the activity carried out by crowdfunding platforms and verifies the presence of the aforementioned requirements.

A list of 13 Spanish equity crowdfunding platforms can be found on the CNMV official website. All platforms are local (i.e., headquartered in Spain). Most of the platforms adopt a hybrid business model, which combines equity-based crowdfunding with other typologies such as lending-based crowdfunding. Only four platforms (i.e., Crowdfunding Bizkaia, Crowdhouse Worldwide, Capital Cell, and Startupxplore) are entirely equity-based crowdfunding platforms. Table 2.3 shows the list of all equity crowdfunding platforms authorised by Spanish law and listed in the CNMV register.

2.6.3 Italy

Under the requirements of Article 50 quinquies 'Management of crowdfunding portals for the collection of capital for small and medium-sized enterprises and social enterprises' of the Italian Consolidated Finance Act (Testo Unico della Finanza or TUF) the managers of equity crowdfunding platforms (other than banks, financial intermediaries, and all companies already authorised to carry out investment services[2]) need to be registered in the ordinary section of a specific register held by the National Commission for the Societies and the Stock Exchange (CONSOB). The Register of Portals' Managers is published on the CONSOB official website. To be enrolled on the CONSOB register, equity crowdfunding platforms must meet the following requirements (see Article 50 quinquies, subparagraph 3 of the TUF): (i) be established as a joint stock company, a limited partnership joint-stock company, a limited liability company, or a mutual company.; (ii) have a legal and administrative headquarters or, for EU subjects, a permanent establishment in Italy; (iii) those who hold control of the platform and the subjects who perform administrative, management, and control functions must possess the requisites of integrity and professionalism established by CONSOB; and (iv) take out professional liability insurance which guarantees adequate protection for customers, according to the criteria established by CONSOB.

CONSOB supervises portal operators to verify compliance with the provisions of the TUF. To this end, it can convene the directors, statutory auditors, and management personnel, request the communication of data and news and the transmission of deeds and documents, setting the relative deadlines, as well as carry out inspections.

A list of 48 Italian equity crowdfunding platforms can be found on the CONSOB official website. All platforms are local (i.e., headquartered in Italy), with the exception of 1001Pact Italy S.r.l (which is a

Table 2.3 List of Spanish equity crowdfunding platforms

Platform	Foundation year	City	Website	Industry focus
Adventures capital PFP, Sociedad Limitada	2017	Santa Cruz de Tenerife	adventurees.com	General
Business Dream Factory PFP, Sociedad Limitada	2019	Telde	bdkapital.es	General
Crowdfunding Bizkaia, PFP, S.L.	2018	Bilbao	crowdfundingbizkaia.com	General
Crowdhouse Worldwide PFP, S.L.	2018	Barcelona	icrowdhouse.com	Real estate
Dozen Investments PFP, S.L.	2017	Madrid	dozeninvestments.com	General
Einicia Crowdfunding PFP, S.L.	2017	Oleiros	einicia.es	General
Fellow Funders	2016	Madrid	fellowfunders.es	General
Flobers Crowdfunding Spain PFP, Sociedad Limitada	2022	Madrid	flobers.com	Renewable energy
La Bolsa Social	2015	Madrid	bolsasocial.com	Social impact start-ups
PFP Capital Cell, S.L.	2017	Barcelona	capitalcell.es	Health and biotechnology
Sociosinversores 2010 PFP, S.L.	2016	Madrid	sociosinversores.com	General
Startupxplore, PFP, S.L.	2017	Valencia	startupxplore.com	Start-ups

Source: Author's elaboration on data from the CNMV official website www.cnmv.es/Portal/Consultas/Plataforma/Financiacion-Participativa-Listado.aspx.

Table 2.4 List of Italian equity crowdfunding platforms

Platform	Foundation year	City	Website	Industry focus
Action Crowd Funding (Action Crowd S.r.l)	2014	Milan	actioncrowdfunding.it	General
Activant S.r.l	2020	Milan	activant.eu	General
Agri4Crowd S.r.l	2021	Milan	agri4crowd.com	Agri-food
Backtowork24 S.r.l	2015	Milan	backtowork24.com	General
Investi-re (Baldi Finance S.p.a)	2015	Milan	investi-re.it	ICT
Bildap S.r.l	2021	Bologna	bildap.it	Real estate
Brickup S.r.l	2021	Milan	brickup.it	Real estate
Build Around S.r.l	2018	Milan	buildaround.eu	Real estate
Clubdeal S.p.a	2017	Milan	clubdealonline.com	General
Concrete S.r.l	2018	Milan	concreteinvesting.com	Real estate
Crowdfundme S.p.a	2014	Milan	crowdfundme.it	General
Crowdinvest S.r.l	2018	Prato	crowdinvestitalia.it	General
Doorway S.r.l	2018	Bologna	doorwayplatform.com	Tech
Ecomill S.r.l	2014	Milano	ecomill.it	Renewable energy
Equifunding S.r.l	2020	Milano	fundyourjump.eu	General
Etianus S.r.l	2020	Francavilla Fontana	fundscovery.com	General
Exre crowdfunding S.r.l	2021	Milan	exrecrowdfunding.it	Real estate
Finanza condivisa S.r.l	2020	Padua	nestmoney.it	General
Firmaid S.r.l	2021	Sant'Omero	firmaid.it	General
Forcrowd S.r.l	2019	Milan	forcrowd.it	General
Foxcrowd S.r.l	2020	Florence	foxcrowd.it	Real estate
Fundera S.r.l	2014	Milan	fundera.it	General
Idea Crowdfunding S.r.l	2017	Rome	ideacrowdfunding.it	General

(Continued)

Table 2.4 (Continued)

Platform	Foundation year	City	Website	Industry focus
Innexta S.C.R.L	2021	Milan	finnexta.it	General
Lifeseeder S.p.a	2018	Rome	lifeseeder.com	Life science
Meridian 180 S.r.l	2019	Bologna	mybestinvest.it	General
MF next equity crowdfunding S.r.l	2014	Civitanova Marche	mfnextequity.it	General
Migliora S.r.l	2021	Milan	2meetebiz.com	General
Muum Lab S.r.l	2014	Lecce	muumlab.com	General
Opstart S.r.l	2015	Bergamo	opstart.it	Innovation and sustainability
Pariter Equity S.r.l	2020	Trento	partierequity.it	Alternative assets
Partner Sin Crowd S.r.l	2021	Genoa	partnersincrowd.it	General
Puzzle Funding S.r.l	2020	Milan	puzzlefunding.com	General
Re-anima S.r.l	2020	Milan	re-anima.com	Sustainable real estate
Reroi S.r.l	2021	Milan	reroi.it	General
Restartup S.r.l	2021	Milan	myrestartup.it	General
Roots Funding S.r.l	2021	Milan	rootfundme.com	General
Siamo Soci S.r.l	2014	Milan	mamacrowd.com	General
Stars Up S.r.l	2013	Livorno	starsup.it	General
Start Funding S.r.l	2019	Lecce	mediterraneacrowd.it	General
The Ing Project S.r.l	2014	Brescia	200crowd.com	ICT
Upsidetown S.r.l	2020	Milan	upsidetown.it	Real estate and green energy
Walliance S.p.a	2017	Trent	walliance.eu	Real estate
We Are Starting S.r.l	2014	Bergamo	wearestarting.it	General
We Deal S.r.l	2019	Milan	hensoo.it	General
Y-Crowd S.r.l	2021	Milan	yeldocrowd.com	Real estate
1001Pact Italy S.r.l (Lita.co)	2018	Turin	it.lita.co	Social and environmental
4Crowd S.p.a	2018	Milan	house4crowd.com	General

Source: Author's elaboration on data from the CONSOB official website www.consob.it/web/consob-and-its-activities/ordinary-section.

Table 2.5 List of equity crowdfunding platforms operating in the United Kingdom

Platform	Foundation year	City	Website	Industry focus
Angels Den	2007	London	angelsden.com	Early-stage businesses
Code investing	2013	London	codeinvesting.com	Small businesses
Crowd for angels	2013	London	crowdforangels.com	General
Crowd2Fund	2013	London	crowd2fund.com	General
Crowdcube	2011	Exeter	crowdcube.com	General
CrowdInvest	2015	London	crowdinvest.com	Start-ups
Dacxi	2017	London	dacxi.com	Tech companies
Ethex	2010	Oxford	ethex.org.uk	Ethical investment
Growth capital ventures	2015	Durham	growthcapitalventures.co.uk	Property and clean energy
GrowthDeck	2015	London	growthdeck.com	General
InvestDen	2014	London	investden.com	General
Seedrs	2012	London	seedrs.com	Start-ups
ShareIn	2014	Edinburgh	sharein.com	General
Syndicate room	2013	Cambridge	syndicateroom.com	Start-ups
Tifosy	2013	London	tifosy.com	Sports
Triodos Crowdfunding	Not available	Bristol	triodoscrowdfunding.co.uk	Social and environmental organisations
VentureFounders	2013	London	venturefounders.co.uk	Tech companies
Volpit	2012	London	volpit.com	General

Source: Author's elaboration on data from 'the 4th European alternative finance benchmarking report' published by the Cambridge Centre for Alternative Finance (Ziegler *et al.*, 2019) and from the UKCFA official website https://www.ukcfa.org.uk/about-us/#members.

foreign platform headquartered in France but operating in other European countries such as Italy and Belgium.[3] The vast majority of platforms operate in northern Italy in the Lombardy region, followed by Emilia Romagna and Lazio. Some of the 48 platforms were established in 2021 and as of the date of this study have not yet published a single campaign. According to the latest Italian report on crowdinvesting by the Polytechnic of Milan (Giudici *et al.*, 2022), Mamacrowd is the platform that has raised the most capital (€83.61 million effective as at 30 June 2022, of which €32.28 million in the last year) followed by Crowdfundme (€71.09 million, which however published the most campaigns ever, i.e., 192) and by Walliance (with €68.46 million). Table 2.4 shows the list of Italian equity crowdfunding platforms.

2.6.4 *The United Kingdom*

In order to operate, equity-based crowdfunding platforms must be authorised by the FCA. Registration in an official national register is not required in the United Kingdom. A list of 18 active equity crowdfunding platforms was constructed from the 'The 4th European alternative finance benchmarking report' published by the Cambridge Centre for Alternative Finance (Ziegler *et al.*, 2019) and from the UK Crowdfunding Association (UKCFA) members list. The platforms have been double-checked on the web in order to select only those based on equity. Table 2.5 shows the list of equity-based crowdfunding platforms operating in the United Kingdom.

Notes

1 Previously the limit for non-professional investors was set at a maximum of €10,000 in a 12-month period.
2 There is a special section of the register of portal managers dedicated to companies authorised to carry out investment activities that intend to start managing an online portal for the collection of capital. At the moment there are no portal managers registered in the special section of the CONSOB register.
3 The European passport regime allows both lending-based and investment-based crowdfunding platforms to operate at the European level.

References

Block, J. H., Colombo, M. G., Cumming, D. J., & Vismara, S. (2018). New players in entrepreneurial finance and why they are there. *Small Business Economics*, 50, 239–250. 10.1007/s11187-016-9826-6.
Cicchiello, A. F. (2019). Building an entrepreneurial ecosystem based on crowdfunding in Europe: The role of public policy. *Journal of Entrepreneurship and Public Policy*, 8(3), 297–318. 10.1108/JEPP-05-2019-0037.

Cicchiello, A. F. (2020). Harmonizing the crowdfunding regulation in Europe: Need, challenges, and risks. *Journal of Small Business & Entrepreneurship*, 32(6), 585–606. 10.1080/08276331.2019.1603945.

Cicchiello, A. F., & Leone, D. (2020). Encouraging investment in SMEs through equity-based crowdfunding. *International Journal of Globalisation and Small Business*, 11(3), 258–278. 10.1504/IJGSB.2020.109553.

Cicchiello, A. F., Battaglia, F., & Monferrà, S. (2019). Crowdfunding tax incentives in Europe: A comparative analysis. *The European Journal of Finance*, 25(18), 1856–1882. 10.1080/1351847X.2019.1610783.

Cicchiello, A. F., Pietronudo, M. C., Leone, D., & Caporuscio, A. (2020). Entrepreneurial dynamics and investor-oriented approaches for regulating the equity-based crowdfunding. *Journal of Entrepreneurship and Public Policy*, 10(2), 235–260. 10.1108/JEPP-03-2019-0010.

Cumming, D. J., Leboeuf, G., & Schwienbacher, A. (2020). Crowdfunding models: Keep-it-all vs. all-or-nothing. *Financial Management*, 49(2), 331–360. 10.1111/fima.12262.

Estrin, S., Gozman, D., & Khavul, S. (2018). The evolution and adoption of equity crowdfunding: Entrepreneur and investor entry into a new market. *Small Business Economics*, 51, 425–439. 10.1007/s11187-018-0009-5.

European Commission. (2015). Action plan on building a capital markets union. Available at: https://ec.europa.eu/info/publications/action-plan-building-capital-markets-union_en (Retrieved on 24 July 2023).

European Commission. (2016). Commission staff working document on crowdfunding in the EU Capital Markets Union. Available at: https://finance.ec.europa.eu/publications/crowdfunding-eu-capital-markets-union_en (Retrieved on 24 July 2023).

European Commission. (2017a). Report from the Commission to the Council and the European Parliament. Accelerating the capital markets union: Addressing national barriers to capital flows. Available at: https://ec.europa.eu/transparency/documents-register/detail?ref=COM(2017)147&lang=en (Retrieved on 24 July 2023).

European Commission. (2017b). Identifying market and regulatory obstacles to cross-border development of crowdfunding in the EU. Final report December 2017. Available at: https://finance.ec.europa.eu/publications/identifying-market-and-regulatory-obstacles-crossborder-development-crowdfunding-eu_en#files (Retrieved on 24 July 2023).

European Commission. (2018a). FinTech Action Plan: For a more competitive and innovative European financial sector. Available at: https://eur-lex.europa.eu/legal-content/EN/TXT/?uri=CELEX%3A52018DC0109 (Retrieved on 24 July 2023).

European Commission. (2018b). Proposal for a regulation of the European Parliament and of the Council on European Crowdfunding Service Providers (ECSP) for Business. Available at: https://eur-lex.europa.eu/legal-content/EN/TXT/?uri=celex%3A52018PC0113 (Retrieved on 24 July 2023).

European Union. (2020). Regulation (EU) 2020/1503 of the European Parliament and of the Council of 7 October 2020 on European crowdfunding service providers for business, and amending Regulation (EU) 2017/1129 and Directive (EU) 2019/1937. Available at: https://eur-lex.europa.eu/legal-content/EN/TXT/?uri=CELEX%3A32020R1503 (Retrieved on 24 July 2023).

Gabison, G. A. (2014). Equity crowdfunding: All regulated but not equal. *DePaul Business and Commercial Law Journal*, 13(3), 359–409.

Giudici, G., Conti, M., Giordano, F., Leonardi, G., Mazzucco, L., Mearelli, E., ... & Zaccagnino, M. (2022). 7° Report italiano sul CrowdInvesting. Osservatori Entrepreneurship Finance & Innovation. *Politecnico di Milano*. Available at: https://www.osservatoriefi.it/efi/wp-content/uploads/2022/07/reportcrowd2022.pdf (Retrieved on 05 April 2023).

Hornuf, L., Klöhn, L., & Schilling, T. (2018). Financial contracting in crowdinvesting: Lessons from the German market. *German Law Journal*, 19(3), 509–578. 10.1017/S2071832200022781.

Löher, J. (2019). The interaction of equity crowdfunding platforms and ventures: An analysis of the preselection process. In C. Bellavitis, I. Filatotchev, D. S. Kamuriwo, & T. Vanacker (eds.), *Entrepreneurial Finance: New Frontiers of Research and Practice* (pp. 51–74). London: Routledge. 10.4324/9781351202152.

Mollick, E. (2014). The dynamics of crowdfunding: An exploratory study. *Journal of Business Venturing*, 29(1), 1–16. 10.1016/j.jbusvent.2013.06.005.

Schwienbacher, A., & Larralde, B. (2010). Crowdfunding of small entrepreneurial ventures. In D. Cumming (ed.), *The Oxford Handbook of Entrepreneurial Finance*. New York, NY: Oxford University Press, pp. 369–391. 10.2139/ssrn.1699183.

Signori, A., & Vismara, S. (2018). Does success bring success? The post-offering lives of equity-crowdfunded firms. *Journal of Corporate Finance*, 50, 575–591. 10.1016/j.jcorpfin.2017.10.018.

Vulkan, N., Åstebro, T., & Sierra, M. F. (2016). Equity crowdfunding: A new phenomena. *Journal of Business Venturing Insights*, 5, 37–49. 10.1016/j.jbvi.2016.02.001.

Walthoff-Borm, X., Vanacker, T. R., & Collewaert, V. (2018). Equity crowdfunding, shareholder structures, and firm performance. *Corporate Governance: An International Review*, 26(5), 314–330. 10.1111/corg.12259.

Ziegler, T., Shneor, R., Wenzlaff, K., Odorovic, A., Johanson, D., Hao, R., & Ryll, L. (2019). The 4th European alternative finance benchmarking report. Cambridge Center for Alternative Finance, Cambridge. Available at https://www.jbs.cam.ac.uk/faculty-research/centres/alternative-finance/publications/ (Retrieved on 13 January 2023).

Ziegler, T., Shneor, R., Wenzlaff, K., Suresh, K., Paes, F. F. D. C., Mammadova, L., ... & Knaup, C. (2021). The 2nd global alternative finance market benchmarking report. *Cambridge Centre for Alternative Finance*. Available at: https://www.jbs.cam.ac.uk/faculty-research/centres/alternative-finance/publications/the-2nd-global-alternative-finance-market-benchmarking-report/ (Retrieved on 18 January 2023).

3 Loan-based crowdfunding

An alternative funding channel to credit intermediaries

3.1 Introduction

Peer-to-peer (P2P) lending has emerged as a potential alternative to traditional financing where money is provided directly by investors to fund seekers via an online platform without the need for intermediation from a bank or other financial institution. P2P lending is one of the characteristic financial forms in digital lending in which the lending process is completely managed through digital channels (Murinde *et al.*, 2022). In this type of crowdfunding, investors become creditors by financing borrowers (individuals or companies) in exchange for a financial return in the form of periodic interest and principal at the end of the lending period. The main actors involved in the investment process are (i) lenders (i.e., small-to-medium investors or institutional investors who invest their savings seeking adequate returns on their investment); (ii) borrowers (i.e., individuals or companies, either start-ups or existing companies, seeking to cover their consumption or investment financial needs); and (iii) the P2P lending platforms (i.e., online marketplaces that pool financial resources from lenders and issue loans to borrowers). The fundamental nature of P2P lending crowdfunding is therefore the direct finance that allows individuals and companies to lend and borrow money through online platforms by eliminating banks or other intermediaries (financial disintermediation). P2P lending is supported by a large number of diversified investors who are willing to absorb the credit risks and uncertainties that arise from the information asymmetry problems of adverse selection and moral hazard. Digital lending activities, including P2P lending, are characterised by information asymmetries as borrowers may not provide enough information to allow lenders to make informed investment decisions. As such, P2P lending platforms play a crucial role in performing an efficient borrowers' selection process (ex-ante screening) and in providing updated information throughout the life of the loan (ex-post monitoring). P2P lending is eroding the monopolistic/oligopolistic market for

DOI: 10.4324/9781003381518-4

lending, dominated so far exclusively by commercial banks, making it accessible to everyone. It is working as a tool for financial inclusion, providing 'less bankable' individuals and companies with the opportunities to raise fund.

3.2 How it works

Loan-based crowdfunding models, usually referred to as P2P lending or marketplace lending models,[1] include platforms that enable online lending activities between individual or institutional investors and consumer or business borrowers. As for the other crowdfunding models, lending activities are carried out mostly online through the platforms' websites that connect borrowers with lenders. In order to take part in the lending activity, both borrowers and lenders need to register by creating an account on the platform's website. Borrowers submit loan applications together with all information about their credit history, specifying the conditions required for the loan (e.g., the amount, interest rate, repayment term, and date). Each funding proposal undergoes an extensive internal assessment by the platform supported by all available external data sources such as insolvency registry and credit bureaus. If the loan application is approved, the platform assigns a credit score and an interest rate based on the borrower's ability and willingness to repay the loan. The loan request is then published on the platform's website together with all the personal information about the borrower and the terms of the loan. Investors browse through loan applications and make their investment decisions based on the disclosed information. As lending platforms operate according to 'All Or Nothing' (AON) approach, if the entire loan amount is not collected within the set deadline, the loan application is cancelled and all raised funds are returned to the investors. On the contrary, if the whole loan amount is raised within the set time, the borrower receives the loan in exchange of the commitment to reimburse it on time with interests. Platform acts as an intermediary, distributing the principal and interest payments among investors and deducting its fees.

Loan-based crowdfunding model offers borrowers (i.e., consumers or businesses seeking to cover their financial needs for consumption or investment) more speed and flexibility in accessing loans as the involvement of a financial institution is not required, as well as the opportunity to receive better financial terms and conditions than those normally offered by traditional credit providers (Lenz, 2016). On the lenders' side (i.e., individuals or institutional investors looking for opportunities to invest their financial savings/surplus with the expectation of adequate returns), P2P lending crowdfunding represents an alternative investment solution to those offered by traditional intermediaries. It offers investors the opportunity to fully customise and diversify their investment portfolio and lend a flexible loan amount over a specified time horizon to local businesses and socially and environmentally responsible projects while offering higher returns (Bachmann *et al.*, 2011).

Where permissible under applicable regulations, platforms can provide, in exchange for a sales fee, liquidity services by creating secondary markets (so-called bulletin boards) where lenders can sell their loans to other investors. Depending on market supply and demand, the sale of a loan can be done with a premium or at a discount. Some platforms allow the sale of defaulted loans (Havrylchyk and Verdier, 2018).

Loans provided on crowdlending platforms can take the form of secured loans, against fixed assets such as properties or business assets, or unsecured loans, bonds, or another type of debt-based securities. Some countries such as France allowed the issuance of state-guaranteed loans to overcome the COVID-19 crisis (Kleverlaan *et al.*, 2021).

When the loan is granted to a consumer borrower, the crowdfunding model is called P2P consumer lending, while when the loan is granted to a business, the crowdfunding model is called P2P business lending. This chapter focuses on the provision of business loans through crowdfunding platforms as it represents an important (and sometimes the only) alternative financing channel for European micro, small, and medium-sized enterprises (MSMEs) and start-ups that are rationed by the financial system as they are considered informatively opaque (Mc Namara *et al.*, 2020).

P2P lending platforms (both business and consumer) generally operate on an 'off-balance-sheet' (OBS) accounting practice, which means that they do not provide loans directly to borrowers but simply act as intermediaries (or marketplaces) that facilitate online lending to businesses or consumers. According to this practice, the platform does not include the liabilities on its balance sheet. In this way, if the loan is not repaid, the risk of financial loss would fall on the investor and not on the platform. On the contrary, lending platforms operating on an 'on-balance-sheet' accounting practice, act as non-bank credit intermediaries originating and directly funding consumer or business loans using funds from their balance sheet. In this case, if the loan is not repaid, the risk of financial loss would fall entirely on the platform.

According to a recent study by Cambridge Center for Alternative Finance (Ziegler *et al.*, 2019), lending platforms can be divided into three categories depending on the borrowers they are addressed to. The first category includes lending platforms focused on consumers (i.e., individuals or households). This category includes (i) OBS P2P consumer lending (i.e., the platform acts as an intermediary between individuals or institutional lenders and consumer borrowers); (ii) on-balance-sheet consumer lending (i.e., the platform delivers loans directly to consumer borrowers); and (iii) customer cash advance or buy now/pay later – BNPL – (i.e., the platform acts as a buy now/pay later payment facilitator or a store credit solution). The second category includes lending platforms focused on businesses (i.e., MSMEs, start-ups, or other business entities). This category includes: (i) OBS P2P business lending (i.e., the platform acts as an intermediary between individuals or institutional lenders and business borrowers); (ii) on-balance-sheet business lending (i.e., the platform delivers loans directly to business borrowers); (iii) invoice trading (i.e., the platform acts as an intermediary between individuals or institutional funders, who purchase discounted invoices or receivable notes, and businesses); and (iv) merchant cash advance (i.e., the platform acts as an intermediary between retail and/or institutional investors, who provide cash advances, and businesses, who repay lenders through fixed payments or through future payments based on sales, plus a small fee).

The third category includes hybrid lending platforms that focus both on consumers (i.e., individuals or households) and businesses (i.e., MSMEs, start-ups, or other business entities). This category includes: (i) OBS P2P property lending (i.e., the platform acts as an intermediary between individuals or institutional lenders and consumer or business borrowers for loans secured by a property); (ii) on-balance-sheet property lending (i.e., the platform delivers loans secured by a property directly to consumer or business borrowers); (iii) debt-based securities/debentures[2] (i.e., the platform acts as an intermediary between individuals or institutional funders, who purchase debt-based securities such as bonds or debentures at a fixed interest rate, and businesses); (iv) mini bonds[3] (i.e., the platform acts as an intermediary between individuals or institutional funders, who purchase mini bonds, and businesses); and (v) crowd-led microfinance (in this crowdfunding model loans are provided at lower rates and can also take the form of donations with all interests and/or other profits generated from loans being reinvested in new microcredit, most commonly for pro-social purposes). Lending platforms usually operate in more than one of the models mentioned above.

3.3   Platforms' business models

As reported by Kirby and Worner (2014, pp. 16–19) in a study made for the International Organization of Securities Commissions (IOSCO), P2P lending platforms operate under different business models which can be grouped into three main categories: (i) the client-segregated account model; (ii) the notary model; and (iii) the guaranteed return model. The choice of business models depends on the crowdfunding regulatory system of the country in which the platform operates and the self-regulatory frameworks enshrined in the codes of conduct and ethics enacted by the platforms (Odorović and Wenzlaff, 2020).

3.3.1 The client-segregated account model

The first P2P lending business model is called the 'client-segregated account model' as all funds transferred from lenders to borrowers go through a client-segregated account legally separate from the platforms balance sheet. The existence of a separate account for the funds raised on the platform ensures that the contractual obligations settled directly between lenders and borrowers without the involvement of the platform persist in the event of platform bankruptcy and are protected against any claims for eventual creditor positions of any kind. This model is certainly the one with the lowest degree of involvement of the platform in the lending activity. The platform matches loan requests from borrowers with offers of financial resources from lenders after assessing the creditworthiness of the former and offers administrative services of various kinds. Lenders' funds are allocated automatically based on the platform's random allocation method or manually based on the lenders' own judgement. Unlike banks that earn their profits from the interest spread, platforms earn their profits from fees. Therefore, the platform applies a commission as a percentage on transactions between lenders and borrowers as the fee for intermediation activities conducted through the website. In particular, borrowers are charged an origination fee, which may be a flat fee or determined as a percentage of the loan amount funded, as well as additional unsuccessful payment fees and late payment fees in case of borrower default. Lenders are charged an administration fee for the overall services offered by the platforms, which include, for example, the registration on the platform website, the preliminary assessments on the borrowers' creditworthiness, and the collection of loan repayments. Additional fees are charged if lenders want to trade their investment on the secondary markets offered by the platform. The client-segregated account model can involve the creation of a trust fund where lenders buy fund shares in a trust structure, and the platform acts as a trustee and manages the fund by building a diversified portfolio and investing in accordance with instructions from the lenders. The trust fund is legally separated from the platform itself, protecting the lenders in the case of the platform's bankruptcy. Figure 3.1 summarises the client-segregated account model.

3.3.2 The notary model

This model is more widespread in the United States than in Europe and is based on a collaboration between the platforms and commercial banks. Similar to the client-segregated account model, in the notary model the platform acts as an intermediary between lenders and borrowers by matching the credit offer of the former with the loan requests of the latter. However, once the amount of money required for the loan is reached, the collected amount is transferred to a bank that

Figure 3.1 Client-segregated account model.

Source: Adapted by the author from Kirby and Worner (2014).

issues the loan in exchange of a loan promissory note from the borrower. At the same time, the platform issues a note to the lenders for the value of the funds they have invested (hence the name, notary model). The note must be presented to the borrower at the time of reimbursement. The borrower repays the note to the bank, then the bank transfers the funds to the platform which in turn returns them to the lenders. Since the funds are not deposited in the bank's accounts but transferred to the platform, the credit risk is transferred by the originating bank to the lenders themselves. The notary model has a fee structure identical to that of the previous model. Figure 3.2 summarises the notary model.

3.3.3 The guaranteed return model

The third P2P lending model is called the guaranteed-return model as the platform determines and guarantees the rate of return for the lender's investment. In this model, the platform acts as a full-fledged financial intermediary, matching lenders and borrowers based on the risk-return profile of the former, defining loans' terms and conditions, granting loans directly, managing lenders' repayments, and setting guaranteed return rates for lenders. This model is widespread in China where some of the largest P2P lending platforms guarantee lenders' capital and offer fixed returns on capital, regardless of the risk level of the loan. In

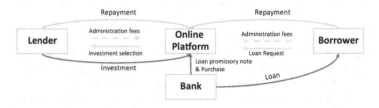

Figure 3.2 Notary model.

Source: Adapted by the author from Kirby and Worner (2014).

Figure 3.3 Guaranteed return model.
Source: Adapted by the author from Kirby and Worner (2014).

Europe, the Swedish platform TrustBuddy International AB, the first-ever P2P lending platform to achieve a stock-market listing on the NASDAQ OMX First North since 2011, has adopted this type of business model, guaranteeing lenders a 12% return. The platform was dissolved in 2016. In a variation of the guaranteed return model, the first phases of the lending activity (e.g., the matching of lenders and borrowers and the assessment of borrowers' creditworthiness) are conducted off-line, through financial consultancy desks or networks. Figure 3.3 summarises the guaranteed return model.

3.4 The regulatory context

Over the last years, P2P lending crowdfunding has become a significant alternative funding channel offering start-ups and SMEs the opportunity to finance their projects. European countries have approached crowdfunding regulation very differently, modelling their internal regulations based on the characteristics and needs of local markets and investors. Some countries have issued tailor-made regulations, also relating to the different forms of crowdfunding. Other countries have improved the flexibility and reach of existing regulatory frameworks, filled gaps within them, and adapted them in response to the challenges posed by crowdfunding (Cicchiello, 2019).

To counter the excessive fragmentation of the regulatory frameworks on crowdfunding of individual Member States, the European Commission has started a process of regulatory harmonisation (for further details, see Cicchiello, 2020) and the definition of European standards in terms of platform disclosure. As part of this process, the European Commission issued Regulation (EU) 2020/1503 of the European Parliament and of the Council of 7 October 2020 on European crowdfunding service providers (CSPs) for business (ECSP regulation), and amending Regulation (EU) 2017/1129 and Directive (EU) 2019/1937.[4] The Regulation was accompanied by Directive (EU) 2020/1504 amending directive 2014/65 EU on markets in financial instruments (MiFID II). Both the Regulation and Directive entered into force on 9 November 2020.

Regulation (EU) 2020/1503 facilitates the cross-border provision of crowdfunding services by establishing uniform operational and organisational requirements and a single European authorisation. In this way, once authorised by the national competent authority as CSPs, the platforms can freely provide their services throughout the territory of the European Union, in accordance with the European Regulation and without the need to obtain a different authorisation in each Member State where they intend to provide their services. The national agencies, such as the Central Banks or the Securities Markets Offices, are in charge of supervising the activity of the platforms. The regulation establishes a distinction between sophisticated and non-sophisticated investors and introduces different levels of investor protection for each of those categories. Both categories of investors are not subject to any particular investment restrictions, but platforms have to ensure that non-sophisticated investors are aware of the risks of crowdfunding. Regulation also establishes that the maximum amount of funds that can be raised for a project owner through each of the platforms cannot exceed €5,000,000 in a period of 12 months for all types of investors. That threshold can be exceeded up to the limit established in the legislation of each Member State. However, the exemption from the obligation to publish a prospectus in accordance with Regulation (EU) 2017/1129 of the European Parliament and of the Council (the Prospectus Regulation) does not apply in this case. Platforms must be registered in the European Securities and Markets Authority (ESMA) register, which is publicly available on its website and is updated regularly. Regulation allows lending-based crowdfunding platforms to intermediate loans without a banking license and manage an individual portfolio of loans on behalf of the investors. Additionally, they can manage a bulletin board where investors can buy or sell loans or securities originally offered on the platform.

The European Securities and Markets Authority (ESMA) has recently approved two draft regulatory technical standards (RTSs) on crowdfunding (ESMA, 2021), and the European Banking Authority (EBA) has started a consultation on 'credit scoring and loan pricing disclosure, credit risk assessment and risk management requirements for crowdfunding service providers under Article 19(7) Regulation (EU) 2020/1503' (EBA, 2022). The RTSs aim to reduce information asymmetries to the detriment of investors in lending-based crowdfunding in order to strengthen this form of financing while ensuring adequate amounts of information are disclosed by CSPs.

The RTSs are aimed at:

a Reducing potential asymmetries of information between project owners, crowdfunding service providers and investors with respect to credit scoring and loan pricing.

Unlike traditional intermediaries who bear the credit risk by absorbing, at least in part, any losses through their own capital, lending-based crowdfunding platforms do not assume responsibility related to investment decisions made by lenders. Such risk-taking needs to be supported by the provision of an adequate amount of information enabling lenders to properly assess the ability of borrowers to repay debt and, therefore, to make quality investment decisions.

The RTSs are intended to elaborate the requirements that platforms must comply with in order to produce all the information investors need to make an informed investment decision, including the presentation of certain risks, financial ratios, and costs and charges. According to the RTSs, platforms must inform investors on the existence of robust credit scoring processes that allow each project owner to be assigned to a risk category reflecting its inherent credit risk. The platforms are asked to describe the credit score calculation method by indicating i) the methodology employed (i.e., the models), ii) the input to these models (i.e., the information and factors to be considered), and iii) the output of these scoring models.

b Ensuring a minimum set of common standards in terms of credit risk assessment, governance, and risk management structures (internal governance).

The RTSs allow crowdfunding platforms to adopt their own methodology for assessing credit risk as long as this is done on the basis of consistent standards and complete information on the loan so that investors can compare the different loans offered and choose the one best suited to their risk-return profile.

While the EBA's RTSs are aimed at increasing investor protection by ensuring a higher degree of information disclosure, there is a risk that increased transparency requirements on platforms could have a negative impact on crowdfunding transaction volumes. The objective of the lending-based crowdfunding platforms is to offer companies an alternative financing channel to traditional credit institutions based on an almost totally digitised credit supplying process characterised by cost savings and reduced disbursement times. However, if on the one hand the lending-based platforms reduce the costs and times of the credit supplying process, on the other hand they offer extremely standardised and therefore less flexible loan agreements and do not provide any guarantees or protections to lenders who have to bear all risks. In light of the above, it is essential that the technical standards proposed by the EBA increase the degree of investor protection – containing the main risks associated with lending crowdfunding – without creating excessive barriers to entry for platforms.

3.5   Tax relief

To boost crowdfunding investments and offer a counterweight to its risks, European policy makers have set up targeted tax incentive schemes over the years (for more details, see Cicchiello *et al.*, 2019). While most of these schemes target the equity-based crowdfunding model, some have been created specifically for lending activities. The following subparagraphs describe the tax incentive schemes for lending-based crowdfunding in force in France, the United Kingdom, and Belgium (the only countries that adopt tax incentives to encourage P2P lending crowdfunding). Table 3.1 provides an overview of the tax incentive schemes in force in the analysed countries.

3.5.1   *France*

To encourage the lending activity through crowdfunding platforms, French legislation has provided for a loss allocation system starting from 1 January 2016. Article 25 of the Amended Finance Act for 2015 n° 2015–1786, of 29 December 2015 (Loi de Finance Rectificative

Table 3.1 Overview of the tax incentive schemes in force in the analysed countries.

Country	Incentive scheme	Benefits
France	Losses allocation	Lenders can impute the capital losses on unrepaid loans on interest generated by other loans granted during the same year or in the five years following.
United Kingdom	Innovative Finance ISA Scheme (IFISA)	Tax free interest and capital gains on money lend through FCA-regulated and approved P2P crowdfunding platforms, up to the limit of £20,000 for 2022/23 financial year.
		Lenders can offset the losses they suffer on the unpaid loans against the interest they receive on other P2P loans before the income is taxed.
Belgium	Tax exemption	Lenders benefit from a withholding tax exemption on 30% of the annual interest income received for loans in start-up companies through P2P lending platforms up to a maximum of €30,000.

Source: Author's elaboration.

pour 2015, LFR) allows lenders acting as natural persons to deduct capital losses suffered in case of default on loan repayments from the interest generated by all loans granted on crowdfunding platforms during the same year or in the subsequent five years with a limit of €2,000 per financed company (Code général des impôts – CGI – Article 125–00A).

Article 44 of the Amended Finance Act for 2016 n° 2016–1918, of 29 December 2016 (Loi de Finance Rectificative pour 2016, LFR) has extended the benefit of the losses allocation system to the mini-bonds subscribed from 1 January 2017. Furthermore, it has established a ceiling of €8,000 for the losses deductible in the year. If the ceiling of €8,000 is exceeded, the losses incurred can be charged against the interest generated by the loans in the following five years.

3.5.2 The United Kingdom

To encourage low- and middle-income households to save more money, the UK government set up Individual Savings Accounts (ISAs) in 1999. ISAs are tax-free savings accounts that allow individuals aged 18 or over who are residents and ordinarily residents in the United Kingdom to invest up to a pre-set limit in each tax year (so-called 'ISA allowance') and protect any returns or capital gains made with money placed in an ISA from the income and capital gains tax. People do not even need to declare ISAs on their tax returns. There are four types of ISA available: (i) cash ISAs (include savings in banks and building society accounts and some national savings and investment products); (ii) stocks and shares ISAs (include shares in companies, unit trusts, and investment funds, corporate bonds, and government bonds); (iii) lifetime ISAs (include the first home purchase or future life savings); and (iv) innovative finance ISAs (IFISAs). The government provides a Junior ISA for UK resident children under the age of 18 who do not have a Child Trust Fund account.

IFISAs were introduced in April 2016 and allow individuals to use some (or all) of their annual ISA allowance to lend funds through loan-based crowdfunding platforms or P2P lending platforms on an income-tax-free basis. To be eligible, platforms must be regulated and approved by the Financial Conduct Authority (FCA). Investors can choose to split their annual ISA allowance (£20,000 for the 2022/23 financial year) into one or more ISAs. As in France, UK lenders can offset losses incurred on unpaid loans against the interest earned on other P2P loans before income tax is charged. Tax relief allows a 12-month carry-back and applies only if there is no reasonable possibility that the P2P loan will be repaid. It does not apply to late payments. In order for the bad debt tax relief to apply, the lender must be a UK tax resident, and the bad debt loan must have taken place on an FCA-authorised P2P lending platform.

3.5.3 Belgium

To promote investment in crowdlending, Belgian legislation provides lenders with a withholding tax exemption on 30% of the annual interest income received for loans in start-up companies through P2P lending platforms recognised by the Authority for Financial Services and Markets (FSMA) up to a maximum of €30,000. According to the Belgian Law on crowdfunding platforms of 18 December 2016, to be eligible for this scheme, lenders must be Belgian individual taxpayers, and the loan must meet the following conditions:

- it must have a maturity of at least four years;
- it must be invested in a start-up that is less than four years old;
- it cannot be used for refinancing.

3.6   Key players in P2P business lending market

The P2P business lending market has expanded significantly around Europe (excluding the United Kingdom) in recent years, growing from $52 million in 2013 to $1,844 million in 2020 (Ziegler *et al.*, 2021). It currently represents the third largest model in Europe after P2P/Marketplace Consumer Lending and the invoice trading. In 2020, the United Kingdom has significantly outperformed other European countries with a market volume of $3,262 million, followed by Italy ($808 million), France ($412 million), and the Netherlands ($214 million). Figure 3.4 shows the P2P business lending market volume in Europe (excluding the United Kingdom) over the time period 2013–2020. Table 3.2 shows the P2P business lending market volume by country over the time period 2015–2020.

The following subparagraphs report a list of the key players in P2P business lending market within four representative countries in Europe (i.e., France, Spain, the United Kingdom, and Italy). P2P business lending platforms operating in the real estate industry were excluded. These countries were selected based on data availability and the fact that they all have a relatively large P2P business lending market volume compared to other European countries and a much more mature crowdfunding ecosystem. Germany was excluded as the websites of the platforms are in German, and therefore it was not possible to collect information on the general conditions of the loans.

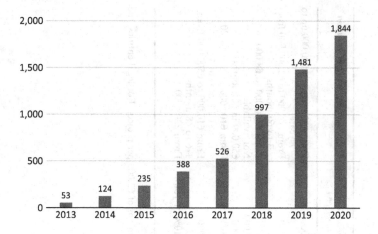

Figure 3.4 P2P business lending market volume in Europe (excluding the United Kingdom) 2013–2020 (USD, millions).

Source: Author's elaboration on data from Ziegler *et al.* (2021).

Table 3.2 P2P business lending market value by country 2015–2020 (USD, millions)

	2015	2016	2017	2018	2019	2020
The United Kingdom	1148.7	1606.3	2658.5	2541.9	2538	3262
Germany	53.15	25.4	77.93	161.8	n/a	n/a
France	30.78	77.38	95.72	148.1	159	412
Netherlands	73.95	144.15	94.37	147.5	286	214
Spain	21.8	48.6	46.6	93.5	90.3	53.8
Italy	0.65	6.6	26.19	75.9	600	808

Source: Author's elaboration on data from Ziegler *et al.* (2021) and Kleverlaan *et al.* (2021).
Note: Since the German Credit Platforms Association (VdK – Verband deutscher Kreditplattformen) has not published any data regarding lending-based crowdfunding in Germany, data for the years 2019 and 2020 is missing.

3.6.1 *France*

In France all lending-based platforms shall be listed in the official register of the French association ORIAS (*Registre Unique des Intermédiaires en Assurance Banque et Finance*) as a 'Intermédiaire en Financement Participatif' (IFP). The list of all French P2P business lending platforms is available on the ORIAS website and includes all platforms licensed under French regulation. Table 3.3 shows the list of all P2P business lending platforms authorised by French law and listed in the ORIAS register.

Table 3.3 List of French P2P business lending platforms

Platform	Foundation year	City	Origination fee	Min. and max. amount that can be invested per project (*)	Max. loan amount and duration
October	2014	Paris	3%	From €20 to €2,000	From €30,000 to €5,000,000 up to 7 years
Credit.fr	2014	Levallois-perret	4%	From €50 to €2,000	From €20,000 to €2,500,000 from 3 to 60 months
Wiseed	2008	Toulouse	5% to 10%	From €100	From €300,000 to €8,000,000
Bolden	2014	Paris	4%	From €100 to €2,000	Not available
Bienprêter	2017	Paris	1.20% to 3.90%	From €20 to €2,000	€50,000 in 60 months
Clubfunding	2014	Paris	5% to 7%	From €1,000 to 10% of your total assets	From €100,000 to €8,000,000 from 6 months to 4 years
Unilend (pretup)	2013	Paris	3% to 5%	From €20 to €2,000	From €10,000 to €500,000 from 6 to 48 months
Finple	2013	Nantes	4% to 7%	From €1,000 to 10% of your total assets	From €200,000

Source: Author's elaboration on data from ORIAS.
(*) The French regulation sets a total limit of €1,000,000 for natural persons with a maximum of €2,000 per project. For legal entities, the regulatory limit is €2,500,000 per project.

3.6.2 Spain

According to Article 46 of Law 5/2015 for the Promotion of Business Financing (*Ley de Fomento de la Financiación Empresarial*, also called LFFE), crowdfunding platforms must be authorised by the Spanish Securities Market Commission (*Comision Nacional del Mercado de Valores*, CNMV) and listed in its official register. To be enroled in CNMV registry, platforms must meet high capital and financial requirements established by the LFFE (Articles 55 and 56). Table 3.4 shows the list of all P2P business lending platforms authorised by Spanish law and listed in the CNMV register.

3.6.3 Italy

Registration in an official national register is not required in Italy. A list of 12 Italian P2P business lending platforms can be found on the annual Italian Report on CrowdInvesting published by the Entrepreneurship Finance and Innovation Observatories (Giudici *et al.*, 2022) by the Politecnico of Milan. All platforms are local (i.e., headquartered in Italy), with the exception of October which is a foreign platform headquartered in France but operating in other European countries such as Italy, Spain, Holland, and Germany. Two of the 12 platforms (namely, Longevy and The Art Finance) were established in 2021, and as of the date of this study still do not have any successful campaigns. Trust me and Opyn platforms do not raise from the crowd but only from professional investors. Table 3.5 shows the list of Italian P2P business lending platforms.

3.6.4 The United Kingdom

Registration in an official national register is not required in the United Kingdom. A list of 13 P2P business lending platforms can be found on the website P2P Market Data,[5] a platforms' data aggregator.

The 12 platforms extracted from the website P2P Market Data have been double-checked with those listed on the website 4thway.co.uk, a crowdfunding platform comparator.[6] From this website five platforms have been added (namely, Money & Co, Market Finance, Rockpool, Share Credit, and Qardus), resulting in a final list of 17 P2P business lending platforms. Since December 2022 the Assetz Capital and ArchOver platforms are no longer open to investment from individual investors but are only financed by institutional investors. Table 3.6 shows the list of P2P business lending platforms operating in the United Kingdom.

Table 3.4 List of Spanish P2P business lending platforms

Platform	Foundation year	City	Origination fee	Min. and max. amount that can be invested*	Max. loan amount and duration
MytripleA	2016	Golmayo	2%	From €50 to €3,000 per project or €10,000 in 12 months	From €50,000 to €2,000,000 from 1 month to 5 years
Adventurees capital	2017	Santa Cruz de Tenerife	1.5%	Max. €3,000 per project or €10,000 in 12 months	Max. €2,000,000 or €5,000,000 for projects financed exclusively by accredited investors
Business dream factory	2019	Telde	2% to 5%	From €1,000 to €3,000 per project or €10,000 12 months	Max. €2,000,000 or €5,000,000 for projects financed exclusively by accredited investors
Criptalia	2020	Barcelona	3% to 5%	From €20 to €3,000 per project or €10,000 12 months	From €35,000 to €5,000,000 from 4 months to 5 years
Dozen investments	2017	Madrid	6%	from €1,000 to €3,000 per project or €10,000 12 months	€50,000 in 60 months
Ecrowdl (Ecrowd invest)	2016	Barcelona	1%	From €50 to €3,000 per project or €10,000 in 12 months	From €25,000 to €300,000
Einicia	2017	Oleiros	2% to 10%	from €20 to €3,000 per project or €10,000 in 12 months	From €10,000 to €500,000 from 6 to 48 months
Gedesclub	2020	Valencia	5%	No limits. The platform is only for accredited investors	From €50,000 to €5,000,000 from 1 month to 5 years

October España	2016	Madrid	3%	From €20 to €2,000	From €30,000 to €5,000,000 up to 7 years
Socilen	2016	Logroño	2% to 5%	From €20 to €3,000 per project or €10,000 in 12 months	From €1,000 to €900,000 from 1 month to 5 years
Colectual	2016	Valencia	2.25%	From €100 to €3,000 per project or €10,000 in 12 months	From €10,000 to €5,000,000 from 1 month to 48 months
Stockcrowd	2018	Madrid	3%	from €20 to €3,000 per project or €10,000 in 12 months	From €6,000 to €5,000,000 from 1 month to 48 months

Source: Author's elaboration on data from the Spanish Securities Market Commission (CNMV) registry.

Notes
* There are no investment limits for accredited investors.

Table 3.5 List of Italian P2P business lending platforms

Platform	Foundation year	City	Website	Industry focus
Business Lending (Europay S.r.l)	2016	Udine	businesslending.it	General
Credimi S.p.a(*)	2017	Milan	credimi.com	General
CrowdLender (Opstart S.r.l)	2015	Bergamo	crowdlender.it	General
Ener2Crowd S.r.l	2018	Milan	ener2crowd.com	Renewable Energy
Evenfi (Criptalia S.r.l)	2018	Bergamo	evenfi.com	General
Investimento Digitale S.r.l	2021	Modena	investimentodigitale.it	General
October Italia S.r.l	2016	Milan	it.october.eu	General
Longevy finance S.p.a	2021	Florence	longevy.finance	Healthcare
Optimart S.r.l	2021	Milan	optimart.it	Art
Opyn(*) (Business Innovation Lab S.p.a)	2012	Milan	opyn.eu	General
Profit Farm S.r.l	2020	Milan	profitfarm.it	General
The Art Finance S.p.a	2021	Milan	theartfinance.com	Culture

Source: Author's elaboration on data from the annual Italian Report on CrowdInvesting. (*) Collection via web currently not active in Italy.

Table 3.6 List of P2P business lending platforms operating in the United Kingdom

Platform	Foundation year	City	Website	Industry focus
Assetcapital (Assets SME Capital Ltd)	2013	Manchester	assetzcapital.co.uk	House building and care
ArchOver Ltd	2013	London	archover.com	General
Ablrate (Aviation & Tech Capital Ltd)	2012	London	ablrate.com	General
Crowdstacker Ltd	2014	London	crowdstacker.com	General
Crowd2fund Ldt	2013	London	crowd2fund.com	General
Funding Circle Ltd	2009	London	Fundingcircle.com	General
Funding Knight (Sancus Lending Ltd)	2011	London	Fundingknight.com	General
HNW Lending Ltd	2013	London	hnwlending.co.uk	General
Lendingcrowd Finance Ltd	2014	Edinburgh	lendingcrowd.com	General
Care International UK Ltd	2013	London	lendwithcare.org	Farming and Retail Grocery
Kriya Finance Ltd	2010	London	kriya.com	General
Money&co (Denmark Square Ltd)	2013	London	moneyandco.com	General
Qardus Ltd	2019	London	qardus.com	Healthcare and Manufacturing
Rebuildingsociety.com Ltd	2011	Leeds	rebuildingsociety.com	General
Rockpool Investment Llp	2011	London	rockpool.uk.com	General
Share Credit Ltd	2015	London	sharecredit.co.uk	General
Crowd for Angels UK Ltd	2013	London	crowdforangels.com	General

Source: Author's elaboration.

Notes

1 In some jurisdictions this model is referred to as Collaborative Financing or Crowdlending.
2 Debentures are unsecured debt instruments backed exclusively by the general credit of the borrower, usually a government or large company. For further information on such a financial instrument, see Brigham (1966) or Flannery and Sorescu (1996).
3 Mini bonds are small-size debt securities (hence the name, mini bonds) issued by unlisted companies, usually SMEs or start-ups. Unlike traditional corporate bonds listed in institutional capital markets, mini bonds are not always transferable and be held until they mature. Furthermore, mini bonds have an issue size much smaller than the minimum issue amount needed for a traditional bond. For further information on such a financial instrument, see Altman *et al.* (2020) and Mietzner *et al.* (2018).
4 See, https://www.legislation.gov.uk/eur/2020/1503.
5 See https://p2pmarketdata.com/platforms/.
6 See https://www.4thway.co.uk/candid-opinion/peer-to-peer-lending-uk-companies/.

References

Altman, E. I., Esentato, M., & Sabato, G. (2020). Assessing the credit worthiness of Italian SMEs and mini-bond issuers. *Global Finance Journal*, 43, 100450. 10.1016/j.gfj.2018.09.003.

Bachmann, A., Becker, A., Buerckner, D., Hilker, M., Kock, F., Lehmann, M., ... & Funk, B. (2011). Online peer-to-peer lending-a literature review. *Journal of Internet Banking and Commerce*, 16(2), 1. 10.1016/j.elerap.2021.101069.

Brigham, E. F. (1966). An analysis of convertible debentures: Theory and some empirical evidence. *The Journal of Finance*, 21(1), 35–54. 10.1111/j.1540-6261. 1966.tb02953.x.

Cicchiello, A. F. (2019). Building an entrepreneurial ecosystem based on crowdfunding in Europe: The role of public policy. *Journal of Entrepreneurship and Public Policy*, 8(3), 297–318. 10.1108/JEPP-05-2019-0037.

Cicchiello, A. F. (2020). Harmonizing the crowdfunding regulation in Europe: Need, challenges, and risks. *Journal of Small Business & Entrepreneurship*, 32(6), 585–606. 10.1080/08276331.2019.1603945.

Cicchiello, A. F., Battaglia, F., & Monferrà, S. (2019). Crowdfunding tax incentives in Europe: A comparative analysis. *The European Journal of Finance*, 25(18), 1856–1882. 10.1080/1351847X.2019.1610783.

EBA. (2022). Final Report. Draft Regulatory Technical Standards on credit scoring and loan pricing disclosure, credit risk assessment and risk management requirements for Crowdfunding Service Providers under Article 19 (7) Regulation (EU) 2020/1503. Available at: https://www.eba.europa.eu/sites/default/documents/files/document_library/Publications/Draft%20Technical%20Standards/2022/EBA-RTS-2022-05%20RTS%20on%20crowdfunding%20for%20service%20providers/1032645/RTS%20on%20crowdfunding%20for%20service%20providers%20.pdf (Retrieved on 23 January 2023).

ESMA. (2021). Draft technical standards under the European crowdfunding service providers for business Regulation, Document no. 35-42-1183.

Flannery, M. J., & Sorescu, S. M. (1996). Evidence of bank market discipline in subordinated debenture yields: 1983–1991. *The Journal of Finance*, 51(4), 1347–1377. 10.1111/j.1540-6261.1996.tb04072.x.

Giudici, G., Conti, M., Giordano, F., Leonardi, G., Mazzucco, L., Mearelli, E., ... & Zaccagnino, M. (2022). 7° Report italiano sul CrowdInvesting. Osservatori Entrepreneurship Finance & Innovation. *Politecnico di Milano*. Available at: https://www.osservatoriefi.it/efi/wp-content/uploads/2022/07/reportcrowd2022.pdf (Retrieved on 19 January 2023).

Havrylchyk, O., & Verdier, M. (2018). The financial intermediation role of the P2P lending platforms. *Comparative Economic Studies*, 60(1), 115–130. 10.105 7/s41294-017-0045-1.

Kirby, E., & Worner, S. (2014). Crowd-funding: An infant industry growing fast. *IOSCO Research Department*, 1–63.

Kleverlaan, R., Wenzlaff, K., Zhao, Y., van de Glind, P., & Roux, E. (2021). Current State of Crowdfunding in Europe 2021. Available at: https://www.crowdfundinghub.eu/wp-content/uploads/2021/09/CrowdfundingHub-Current-State-of-Crowdfunding-in-Europe-2021.pdf (Retrieved on 18 January 2023).

Lenz, R. (2016). Peer-to-peer lending: Opportunities and risks. *European Journal of Risk Regulation*, 7(4), 688–700. 10.1017/S1867299X00010126.

Mc Namara, A., O'Donohoe, S., & Murro, P. (2020). Lending infrastructure and credit rationing of European SMEs. *The European Journal of Finance*, 26(7–8), 728–745. 10.1080/1351847X.2019.1637357.

Mietzner, M., Proelss, J., & Schweizer, D. (2018). Hidden champions or black sheep? The role of underpricing in the German mini-bond market. *Small Business Economics*, 50(2), 375–395. 10.1007/s11187-016-9833-7.

Murinde, V., Rizopoulos, E., & Zachariadis, M. (2022). The impact of the FinTech revolution on the future of banking: Opportunities and risks. *International Review of Financial Analysis*, 81, 102103. 10.1016/j.irfa.2022. 102103.

Odorović, A., & Wenzlaff, K. (2020). The joint production of confidence–self-regulation in European crowdfunding markets. *Baltic Journal of Management*, 15(2), 303–331. 10.1108/BJM-04-2019-0119.

Ziegler, T., Shneor, R., Wenzlaff, K., Odorovic, A., Johanson, D., Hao, R. & Ryll, L. (2019). The 4th European alternative finance benchmarking report. *Cambridge Center for Alternative Finance, Cambridge*. Available at https://www.jbs.cam.ac.uk/faculty-research/centres/alternative-finance/publications/ (Retrieved on 13 January 2023).

Ziegler, T., Shneor, R., Wenzlaff, K., Suresh, K., Paes, F. F. D. C., Mammadova, L., ... & Knaup, C. (2021). The 2nd global alternative finance market benchmarking report. *Cambridge Centre for Alternative Finance*. Available at: https://www.jbs.cam.ac.uk/faculty-research/centres/alternative-finance/publications/the-2nd-global-alternative-finance-market-benchmarking-report/ (Retrieved on 18 January 2023).

4 The impact of crowdfunding on the growth opportunities of European businesses

'Screening' or 'value-added' effect?

4.1 Introduction

As it is well known, young and innovative firms, as well as SMEs, often suffer from financial constraints due to the lack of stable internal cash flow and tangible assets to use as collateral for securing loans and bank debt funding (Beck and Demirguc-Kunt, 2006). Start-ups and smaller companies are indeed characterised by a higher percentage of intangible assets (including worker skills and know-how, business methods, brands, and formal intellectual properties like copyright, patents, and trademarks) that cannot be accurately checked by investors or liquidated (i.e., converted to cash) as quickly as tangible assets and, as such, cannot be pledged as collateral (Hall, 2010). Young innovative firms and SMEs are also more volatile and as such more prone to bankruptcy (Lopez-Gracia and Sogorb-Mira, 2008). In addition, it can be very difficult or expensive for these firms to obtain external financing due to information asymmetries between the firm and potential investors/lenders and the resulted agency problems such as adverse selection and moral hazard (Carpenter and Petersen, 2002; Hall and Lerner, 2010). Banks, as well as financial investors such as business angels and venture capitalists, rely on close and solid relationships with companies to deal with the existence of information problems. According to the relationship banking approach (Uchida *et al.*, 2012), banks can gather relevant information about borrowers' creditworthiness over time by establishing frequent and continuous professional contacts through the provision of various financial services, as well as, personal contacts with them, and their circle of friends and family outside of the financial sphere (Berger and Udell, 1995). This information collected over time, most of which is soft information (i.e., information not readily available in financial statements or public records which is difficult to replicate and transmit outside the bank), allows banks to build up a more complete picture of borrowers, providing useful input into banks' lending decisions. Scholars have shown that relationship lending can be economically beneficial,

DOI: 10.4324/9781003381518-5

especially for opaque firms (Petersen and Rajan, 1994). It can reduce loan pricing, increase the amount and the extension of credit granted, ease up the requirement for collaterals and provide more opportunities for loan workouts when borrowers face financial distress.

Small, micro, and young firms tend to be more informationally opaque than large firms (Cole *et al.*, 2004; Hyytinen and Pajarinen, 2008). This opaqueness makes it difficult for banks to assess whether these firms will be able to generate sufficient cash flows to discharge their debt obligations and/ or will be willing to pay (due to moral hazard behaviours). Opacity problems hamper the financing of SMEs and young companies, reducing their possibility of getting favourable credit terms and conditions. According to the literature (e.g., Hernández-Cánovas and Martínez-Solano, 2010; Moro and Fink, 2013), the negative impact of opaqueness on SME financing can be mitigated through relationship lending. The continuous, personalised, and direct contact with SMEs, their owners, and the local community increases the availability of soft information and enhances credit availability (Behr *et al.*, 2011). According to Diamond (1991), the same may not apply to young firms that do not have long-term lending relationships with banks upon which to build reputational capital. Building on this perspective, several studies in the literature have shown that younger SMEs are more likely to be subject to credit constraints than older SMEs (see, for example, Ferri and Murro, 2015; Kirschenmann, 2016). Difficulties in accessing external capital due to information opacity and associated agency problems have driven demand for alternative sources of financing in both developed and developing countries. Start-ups and early-stage ventures increasingly rely on innovative funding solutions such as crowdfunding instead of turning to traditional bank debt or financial investors such as business angels and venture capitalists (Block *et al.*, 2018).

The pecking order theory of capital structure (Myers and Majluf, 1984) states that, due to information asymmetries and transaction costs, companies tend to establish a hierarchical order when selecting financing options. First, companies will choose to fund their needs by employing internal funds (i.e., retained earnings), when available. Second, in the event that internal funds are not available, companies will choose debt financing (low-risk short-term debt first, high-risk long-term debt later). Finally, they will choose to resort to external equity financing (Lopez-Gracia and Sogorb-Mira, 2008; Serrasquiero *et al.*, 2011). Therefore, companies use the pecking order approach to determine which funding sources best meet their current needs in terms of risk and cost of capital, choosing the cheapest and least risky source first, and the riskiest and more expensive sources as they climb the pecking order. According to Atherton (2012) and Schwienbacher (2013), small businesses and start-ups can use different sources of financing depending on the stage of development they are in.

Drawing on the pecking order theory, some scholars have shown that small businesses turn to crowdfunding only when they have no reasonable opportunities to access other sources of financing. Walthoff-Borm *et al.* (2018), for example, claim that companies only use equity crowdfunding as a 'last resort' when internal funds and debt financing are not available. Similarly, Brown *et al.* (2018, p. 1) provide evidence that equity crowdfunding is the preferred option for *experimental and improvisational entrepreneurs within innovative, consumer-focused, early-stage firms*, many of whom are discouraged borrowers (i.e., entrepreneurs who do not apply for bank loans because they fear their application will be rejected or who have actually received a rejection). In a recent study, Blaseg *et al.* (2020) revealed that entrepreneurs connected to more risky banks are more likely to use equity crowdfunding.

Therefore, according to these authors, crowdfunding is perceived as a substitute relative to traditional sources of entrepreneurial finance to be used only out of necessity as a secondary or backup funding option.

Conversely, other scholars believe that its unique characteristics could allow crowdfunding (in its various forms) to change the way entrepreneurs seek capital, reversing the traditional pecking order (e.g., Drover *et al.*, 2017a; Cummings *et al.*, 2020). Focusing on equity-based crowdfunding, Stevenson *et al.* (2022) find evidence that crowdfunding cannot be considered a 'funding option of last resort' as proposed in prior literature. They argue that in today's dynamic fundraising context – where many more fundraising options exist – firms could base their financing decisions not transactional efficiency but on novel contingency factors such as the creation of nonfinancial value from the funding process itself, the values of external stakeholders, and changing power dynamics. These contingency factors can motivate companies to choose equity crowdfunding, even when other, more consolidated sources of financing are available. Estrin *et al.* (2018) show that in the United Kingdom equity crowdfunding platforms have attracted larger financial flows than existing sources of early-stage entrepreneurial finance such as angel investing or venture capital. Therefore, they argue that for some entrepreneurs, equity crowdfunding could be considered a preferred funding choice rather than a secondary option.

Based on the above, crowdfunding should be considered a complement (and not a substitute) for traditional sources of entrepreneurial finance (Miglo, 2022). Indeed, this new source of capital can be used to successfully start, grow, or sustain new ventures when other sources of financing are not considered appropriate. For instance, entrepreneurs can use crowdfunding to offset the risk of bank loans (Tomczak and Brem, 2013), to retain more control of their ventures (Vismara, 2016), or simply as a bridge capital until the financial credibility gap is closed and business angels and venture capitalists can get involved (Tomczak and Brem, 2013).

4.2 Due diligence process and value-added services

The alternative finance market is constantly evolving, and there are still many aspects and many different players that need to be explored in depth. One of the still open questions in the crowdfunding landscape is whether the success of backed companies – and the consequent investors' returns – are linked to the ability of platforms to select fundraisers by carrying out an effective due diligence process upstream or to the value created downstream by the backers during the investment process.

In the crowdfunding context, due diligence refers to the screening process used by platform managers to evaluate companies and project issuers seeking to raise capital from the crowd. This process is intended to determine which applicants (i.e., project issuers and entrepreneurs) are qualified for a crowdfunding campaign and which are not, so as to eliminate lower quality or fraudulent projects and entrepreneurs. Platform due diligence is performed by collecting and evaluating relevant information about the company's history, its management team, financial statements, its business model, and its market position. Other important information includes the company's credit history, as well as any regulatory or legal issues that could impact its future success and investor's returns. The provided information is usually cross-checked with reliable and independent sources, such as customers and suppliers who have previously interacted with the entrepreneur, to verify its truthfulness.

Due diligence application is extremely resource-intensive and costly to platforms, but it also offers a number of benefits. First, due diligence improves the performance of crowdfunding platforms in terms of a higher percentage of projects successfully funded, a higher number of investors, and a higher amount of capital raised (Cumming *et al.*, 2019a). An effective due diligence process allows platforms to ensure that listed projects are authentic and of high quality and to mitigate potential costs associated with reputational damages and litigation risks associated with low-quality and fraudulent projects. Furthermore, an adequate level of due diligence mitigates information asymmetries between project issuers/ entrepreneurs and investors by encouraging greater transparency and exhaustiveness of the information provided before, during, and after the campaign. Higher-quality campaigns are more likely to be successfully funded as they attract a greater number of investors and capital. The higher the success rate of the projects, the better the reputation of the platform which will therefore be able to attract a greater number of entrepreneurs looking for capital and investors willing to finance them.

It is worth noting that the application of due diligence by crowdfunding platforms does not follow standard guidelines and is extremely flexible compared to that conducted for stock market listing. As a result, it is possible that despite having successfully passed the due diligence process, a large percentage of the listed projects will fail to reach fundraising goals or meet investor expectations (Cumming *et al.*, 2019a). Finally, it should be noted that not all platforms perform due diligence and, among those that undertake this process, there is great variation in the level of depth at which they collect and analyse information.

In addition to due diligence, crowdfunding platforms offer proponents and investors additional value-added services (personalised or not) for the entire duration of the fundraising process (before the launch of the campaign, during, and after) (Rossi and Vismara, 2018). These services include among others: the development of the project's long-term business and financial planning; the promotion of the campaign also through the use of social media; support in presenting the project so that it can appear more attractive; facilitation in the design of crowdfunding contracts; assistance towards potential exit channels.

In light of the above, it is apparent that crowdfunding platforms are not simple intermediaries that connect entrepreneurs (or project issuers) seeking capital to potential investors. They play an active role in the entire fundraising process which goes from checking the quality and veracity of the projects before the start of the campaign, to supporting fundraisers and investors during the campaign through the provision of value-added services and, finally, facilitating the relationship between fundraisers and investors after the campaign has ended (especially for lending-based and equity-based models).

On the supply side, the value created by backers during the fundraising process is not limited to the financial contribution they make to the campaign but also includes other complementary resources that have a strategic value coveted by entrepreneurs. In the context of reward-based crowdfunding, for example, investment intention (i.e., backers' willingness to invest in a project) and feedback intention (i.e., backers' willingness to provide feedback on the product covered by the campaign) play both a fundamental role for the co-creation of value (Su *et al.*, 2021). In addition to providing financial support, backers actively participate in product development and project implementation as value co-creators (Zheng *et al.*, 2018). Investors contribute to the success of the fundraising by sponsoring the project through their social media. Furthermore, they share ideas and early feedback that can help entrepreneurs improve the quality of their products before they are released in the market (Da Cruz, 2018).

In the context of equity-based crowdfunding, in addition to financial support, entrepreneurs often crave the managerial skills inherent in the dispersed crowd of investors (Stevenson *et al.*, 2022). In addition to providing capital that helps companies improve their growth opportunities and financial performance (Eldridge *et al.*, 2019), investors allow entrepreneurs to test their products, develop their brands, and build a loyal customer base (Estrin *et al.*, 2018).

4.3 What happens after? The post-campaign lives of successfully crowdfunded firms

Recent advances in the entrepreneurial finance landscape have highlighted crowdfunding (especially in the forms of equity and lending) as an important financing channel for early-stage innovative ventures and SMEs (Bruton *et al.*, 2015; Block *et al.*, 2018). Despite the growing interest in this segment of the entrepreneurial alternative finance market, there is still no univocal academic support on the influence of crowdfunding activity on the 'post-campaign life' of the backed companies. The informational opacity due to limitations in data availability (Giudici *et al.*, 2020) makes this promising research area still partially unexplored. An intensive debate is thus still open in the entrepreneurial finance literature on the extent to which crowdfunding investments contribute to resolving the financial constraints of the invested companies and improving their growth and future performance (Mochkabadi and Volkmann, 2020). Here, a very important open question needs to be answered: *What happens after a crowdfunding campaign?*

A small but growing body of literature has focused on the outcomes of successful crowdfunding campaigns, measured in terms of successes (or failures) in obtaining subsequent financing (Mochkabadi and Volkmann, 2020).

Drawing on signalling theory (Ross, 1977), prior research has shown that crowdfunding platforms, that have developed a reputation for being good sources of seed funding, can serve as a certification of the quality of ventures that have been seed funded on such platforms (Drover *et al.*, 2017b). This certification mitigates uncertainty associated with early-stage ventures, signalling to the market the quality and potential for success of these ventures and increasing their likelihood of attracting later-stage investors. Thus, crowd-funded firms could be less financially constrained and obtain better conditions in accessing external finance.

Evaluating post-campaign scenarios is critical for the future of crowdfunding markets. Running a successful campaign is only the starting point for companies whose ultimate goal is to build a viable business that can survive and overcome obstacles that may arise, as well as sustain profits over a long period of time (Signori and Vismara, 2018). In the following subparagraphs, post-campaign scenarios and relevant literature on the topic will be examined.

4.3.1 *Seasoned equity crowdfunding offerings and subsequent financing*

A seasoned equity offering (SEO) or capital increase refers to the issuance of additional shares by an already publicly traded company. Just like in the stock market, seasoned equity crowdfunding offerings (SECOs) refer to subsequent equity crowdfunding campaigns after a successful first campaign (Coakley *et al.*, 2022). The term subsequent financing (or follow-up funding) instead includes any other type of financing that a company can obtain after completing (successfully or not) a crowdfunding campaign. Over the last few years, SECOs have assumed growing importance within the equity crowdfunding market. A study from the British Business Bank reported that in 2019 alone, 40% of companies initially financed via crowdfunding platforms raised additional funds through a seasoned equity crowdfunding offering. According to Coakley *et al.* (2022), seasoned equity crowdfunding offerings suffer from fewer information asymmetry problems as investors have at their disposal a greater amount of information relating to the initial campaign and also new information on the performance of the company in the post-campaign period. In one of the first studies, Signori and Vismara (2018) investigate post-campaign scenarios to understand whether (successful) crowdfunding campaigns can transform into successful investment. The authors find evidence that 25.5% of the firms in their sample raised further capital through subsequent equity crowdfunding campaigns on the same platform, and 9.4% received private equity injections from business angels or venture capitalists. The authors also reveal that more dispersed ownership following the initial offering discourages firms from issuing further equity. On the contrary, a faster first fundraising experience encourages firms to return to the platform for a second round of funding.

A successful campaign can also serve as a signal for institutional investors (i.e., business angels and venture capitalists) to provide subsequent financing.

The literature on reward-based crowdfunding provides some evidence that successful crowdfunding campaigns positively affect follow-up funding through the certification effects. Using data from 77,654 successful projects on Kickstarter, Kaminski *et al.* (2019) show that reward-based crowdfunding leads to a subsequent increase in venture capital investments. Instead, according to Ryu *et al.* (2019) successful reward-based crowdfunding campaigns reduce the likelihood of receiving follow-up funding by venture capitalists. Drover *et al.* (2017b) investigate how crowdfunding investments influence the screening process of venture capitalists by certifying venture quality and find that the crowd can produce highly influential certification effects. Using 300 successful campaigns on Kickstarter and Indiegogo, Colombo and Shafi (2021) find evidence that the information provided by crowdfunding campaigns influences the chances to receive external equity capital from professional investors in the aftermath of a campaign.

4.3.2 *Mergers and acquisitions*

Mergers and acquisitions (M&As) are business transactions in which the ownership of companies or their operating units, including all associated

only the organizations themselves are subject to improvement but also the instruments that are used to manage them, including (Wąchol, 2010):

- management concepts – including classical, behavioral, systemic, situational, quantitative, socio-cultural,
- management models – including the rational purpose model, the internal process model, the human relations model, the open systems model, the 7S model,[2]
- management methods – including benchmarking, controlling, lean management, outsourcing, quality management, strategic management, project management, virtual organization, agile organization, innovative organization, process organization, mergers and acquisitions,
- management techniques and management tools – including mathematical, quantitative, qualitative, IT, communication, offensive, system, task-based, comprehensive techniques, e.g., systemic, algorithms, analytical sheets, diagrams, audits.

Among the wide range of tools that are currently used by executives in the process of managing the organization, or more precisely, in the process of its improvement, an audit occupies a special place. In principle, one can put forward the thesis that it is a management instrument that nowadays is not alien to any organization regardless of its size, area, and scope of functioning, as well as the industry in which it operates. Therefore, at this point, the question should be asked: what makes the audit function (especially internal) in an organization so unique? The answer to this question is not so much complex as multithreaded. The point is that the audit – especially an internal audit – can relate to any area of functioning of a given unit. Its scope is virtually unlimited and can also apply to the environment outside the organization. Nevertheless, the importance of the audit against the background of other tools used in the management of the organization is that:

- it provides a holistic approach (holistic and systemic) to assess the state of functioning of the organization,
- it supports and evaluates the management staff in the context of risk management and the correct functioning of the internal control system in the organization,
- it is the third line of defense in risk management and provides an assessment of the processes necessary for the effective functioning of the first and second lines of defense in the organization (see Figure 4.1),
- it provides its main stakeholders with valuable and objective information on the functioning of the organization in terms of financial, operational, managerial, legal, or dealing with risk,

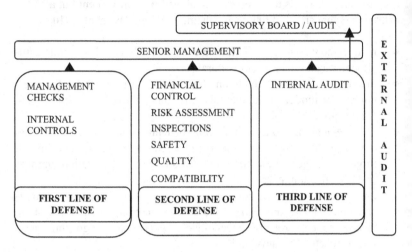

Figure 4.1 Three-line risk defense model from an audit perspective Source: Developed on the basis of the Institute of Internal Auditors.

- it is a provider of advisory services that are designed to improve activities in the organization and contribute to the implementation of its strategic goals.

When taking into account the rare features of the audit compared to other management tools, let us note that through it many areas may be subject to improvement in the organization: financial, technical, operational, as well as organizational, qualitative, or legal issues. What's more – as part of them – both tangible and intangible objects can be improved, which relate directly to (Szczepańska, 2011):

- the organization itself,
- products of the organization's activities (products, services, patents, designs, etc.),
- activities of the organization (work, production, processes),
- elements of the organization (organizational structure, organizational culture, ties, mission, vision, strategic and operational goals),
- relations taking place in the internal and external environment of the organization (relations of the organization with its stakeholders).

The processes of organization improvement carried out as part of the audit may take on various types, which in tabular terms are presented in Table 4.1.

Table 4.1 Improvements – a typology

Criterion	Type of improvement
Durability and continuity	• Continuous (permanent) • Jumping (varied)
Truthfulness (axiological)	• True (real) • Untrue (illusory) • Ethically reprehensible (amoral)
Pattern disclosure	• Standard (with a clearly defined perfect state) • Non-standard (with clearly blurred or default)
Range	• Integrated (holistic, comprehensive) • Disintegrated (fragmentary, sectional)
Reachable	• Unattainable (idealistic) perfection • Achievable (real) perfection

Source: (Skrzypek, 2014, p. 134).

In practical terms, an audit can therefore help an organization to improve and modernize its constituent elements, including:

- atmosphere and organizational culture – by identifying deficiencies and gaps in the assessment of the functioning of a specific culture in the organization, which create the culture: artifacts,[3] value system, principles, norms, views, or behaviors preferred by the organization. Then the audit can take action to strengthen specific behaviors among employees that are close to the values professed in an organization. This approach seems all the more valuable because, in practice, it builds a platform for discussion and dialogue regarding the importance and role of organizational culture in achieving the goals set by the organization, which emerges among employees and between them and management,[4]
- financial and operating results – which in practice may consist of verification of financial statements from previous years. It often happens that errors and weaknesses are then identified, which are revealed in the financial control system of the organization. Thus, audits of performed tasks, or review of completed financial operations, may contribute to increasing the degree of efficiency of both financial results and the operations (processes) themselves,
- internal systems and control mechanisms – mainly due to the fact that the audit does not focus solely on quantifiable and comparable quantities, but also focuses on the general understanding of the systems and control environment that operate in the organization. In this way, deviations in operating systems (accounting, control) are identified, for which instructions can be formulated and proposals for improvements

can be prepared, which will thus contribute to reducing the risk of the business,

- relations with stakeholders – nowadays, due to the high degree of dispersion of shareholders and the growing complexity of integrated supply chains on an international and even global scale, audit may be the only tool that guarantees stakeholders an increase in the degree of transparency of their operations. Audits contribute to increasing the degree of excellence of each organization,

- internal and external security – mainly by examining both technical aspects of network security (firewalls, system construction, algorithm configuration) as well as organizational or human resources security rules. In this type of audits, verification and evaluation, documents regarding both internal and external security procedures, and policies (occurrence of risk factors) applicable in a given organization are also subject to verification and evaluation.

It is understandable that the above-mentioned components of the organization are only a small part of the long list of components that may be subject to effectiveness as a result of the implementation of audit tasks. Nevertheless, the path of implementation of such a process can be both time-consuming and capital-consuming for an organization. What's more, there is no guarantee of success. Paraphrasing Langley et al. (1996), in the context of an integrated approach to process improvement, one can even confirm that any improvement will require change, but not all changes will result in improvement.

In general, regarding the audit approach to organizational improvement presented in this chapter, it should be emphasized that such activities should be defined for different structures and levels of the organization; the more so because these activities properly fit into the concepts of management science, which since its inception – and thus since the birth of the school of scientific management[5] – have placed great emphasis on activities aimed at its improvement. As Cyfert (2006) points out, any omission in the area of organizational improvement, especially in the long term, can lead to serious dysfunctions in the management system, causing the disintegration of processes, procedures, and practices used in the organization.

4.2. Logistics audit in the organization – analysis of the logistics system potential

As part of the managerial assessment of the state of logistics of the enterprise, a logistics audit can also act as a diagnostic tool used to synthetically assess the potential of the entire logistics system. However, the definition of the potential of the logistics system referred to in this book must first be preceded by an explanation of such concepts as analysis, potential, or potential of the system. Therefore, analysis should be understood as a detailed and multi-faceted[6] study of a given phenomenon or problem, the final product of which is the formulation of factual conclusions. As for the word "potential," it is referred to as a resource of possibilities or various types of abilities. In the case of economics, these resources of capabilities, abilities, or performance are most often attributed to given individuals, organizations, groups of people, or systems. As noted by Mastelarz-Kodzis (2018), the size of the potential of a given object or subject can be determined by the set of abilities, competences, skills, and abilities possessed. Not without significance are also qualifications related to the use of these resources, as well as the resources in the environment. Therefore, taking as a criterion the area of occurrence of specific resources of possibilities, we can talk about economic potential, financial potential, market potential, technological potential, or (so popular today) intellectual potential. Having knowledge of what is potential, especially in the context of economic sciences, we can now determine what the potential of the system is.

In this chapter, by potential of the system, we will understand the totality of its possibilities of functioning in accordance with its original purpose. However, it should be mentioned here that the possibilities, capabilities, or resources of the system are not unlimited but are adapted to the given circumstances (boundary conditions). We can now answer the question about the definition of the potential of a logistics system. And so, in broad terms, the potential of the logistics system of the organization can be understood as a force that affects the goals and strategy of the organization. In the case of a narrow approach, we can use the definition proposed by Wasiak (2013), where the potential of the logistics system is understood as its resources and the relations that take place between them, taking into account the principles of work organization, which enable the implementation of specific transformations in the flow of goods and related information. You should be aware that the potential of the organization's logistics system is constantly changing, as a result of changes taking place, for example, among the qualifications and key competences possessed by employees. In addition, as part of a logistics audit, potential can be evaluated using a wide range of measurement methods[7] and techniques related to the overall assessment of the functioning of the logistics system in the organization (see Figure 4.2).

In the context of a holistic assessment of the logistics system, the logistics audit focuses on several important issues:

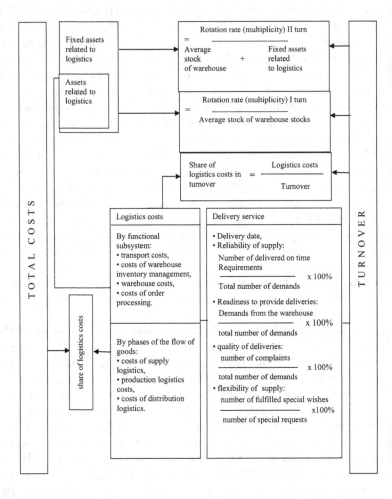

— factually logical dependencies,
→ computational and technical relationships.

Figure 4.2 Holistic assessment of the logistics system – a system of indicators
Source: (Pfohl, 1998, p. 215).

- first, it involves conducting a comparative analysis, which is designed to confront the current state of the logistics system with a set of conditions to be met in a specific organization,
- second, it evaluates the efficiency of the structures and processes of the logistics system, primarily taking into account key processes and

activities that create value, lead time and process costs, involvement of the organization's employees for process improvement and implemented process innovations,

- third, as part of the verification activities, it identifies areas of potential failures and aberrations in the logistics system, in order to improve its quality and systemic efficiency,
- fourth, it creates a management culture based on quality, commitment, and awareness,
- fifth, it provides important information about the logistics system and the existence of potential risk areas.

Bearing in mind the above, in assessing the potential of the company's logistics system, the logistics audit procedure may be helpful, and covers all its most important aspects, and consists of requirements analysis, implementation analysis, process analysis, structure analysis, and comparative analysis (see Table 4.2). In practice, it involves carrying out five stages (Gudehus & Kotzab, 2012):[8]

- in the first stage – requirements analysis aims to define and formulate expectations in the field of logistics services on the part of all stakeholders of the organization. The implementation of this goal is possible mainly thanks to a thorough analysis of available documents and proper assessment of stakeholder requirements. Their capture is made possible by conducting joint interviews with stakeholders, organizing workshops, and creating focus groups, or building prototypes (models, systems, processes). Then, the requirements obtained in this way from our co-operators should be divided into functional, operational, technical, and transitional requirements, in order to be correct in formulating the final conclusions. Finally, all information collected as part of the implementation of individual phases of the requirements analysis must be critically evaluated, due to the need to eliminate those that contradict each other (e.g., demand for better quality of services, for the same money),
- in the second stage – performance analysis examines at what cost, with what efficiency and quality, logistics services are provided. In practice, the results of the conducted research on the efficiency of the logistics system are obtained through data collection, then their transformation and graphic presentation. The data most often comes from profiles, counters, and residual traces of events that have been recorded in the enterprise's logistics system. In contrast, the efficiency of logistics processes, including their quality and productivity, is often assessed using key performance

Table 4.2 Five-stage analysis of the logistics system in the logistics audit

Stage	Type of analysis	Subject of analysis	Problem questions
Stage I	**Requirements analysis**	Conformity requirements	Are the implemented activities consistent with the long-term logistics strategy of the organization?
		Quality requirements	Does the logistics system in the organization ensure the implementation of its strategic, operational, and tactical goals at the level that guarantees the best quality, efficiency and effectiveness?
		Stakeholder requirements	Does the organization have defined needs for the logistics services of its stakeholders?
		Monetary requirements	Does the organization provide services where the relationship is disturbed: more benefits than costs?
		Transformation requirements	What are the possibilities of easy transition from the current state of the organization's logistics system to the planned (new) state?
Stage II	**Performance analysis**	Bottlenecks	Does the organization constantly identify bottlenecks occurring, for example, in the supply chain?
		Where and when tasks are processed	Is the implementation of logistics functions in the organization in accordance with the requirements regarding time, place, and quantity?
		Working time	Is the number of employees employed in the subsystems of the organization's logistics system adequate to the amount of work necessary to be performed?
		Errors and deviations	Are there places in the organization's logistics system where a disproportionate number of errors occur?
		Logistic costs	What logistics costs are generated in the subsystems of the organization's logistics system?

(Continued)

Table 4.2 (Continued)

Stage	Type of analysis	Subject of analysis	Problem questions
Stage III	**Process analysis**	Logistic units	How does the organization of logistics units affect loading in terms of time and finance?
		Master data set	Does the organization have a logistics database and how does it care about their quality?
		Time	Are bottlenecks in the organization identified from the point of view of delivery deadlines?
		Process costs	Does the organization constantly monitor the prices of materials necessary for the production process on the market?
		Stocks	How does an organization control the state and size of its inventory?
		Quality	Does the organization have developed standards and procedures in the field of quality of services provided?
		Process planning and control	How has the scope of work been defined in the organization, for people responsible for planning and controlling logistics processes?
		Supply chain	Have you identified supply chains in your organization that are strategic to your organization?
		Make or Buy (MOB)	Does the organization conduct benchmarking that allows it to solve problems such as: make or buy?
Stage IV	**Structure analysis**	Logistics infrastructure	Is, and how often is, the logistics infrastructure analyzed in the organization in relation to competitors?
		Channels and distribution network	Does the organization identify weak links in distribution channels that are responsible for the movement of tangible and intangible goods?
		Costs of doing business	Are the tasks and the way of organizing work in the organization optimal and does not generate unnecessary costs?

(Continued)

Table 4.2 (Continued)

Stage	Type of analysis	Subject of analysis	Problem questions
Stage V	**Comparative analysis**	Benchmarking	How do the organization's results compare to the competition?
		Case studies	What are the strengths and weaknesses of the organization compared to the industry competition?
		Existing data	What conclusions can the organization draw from an in-depth analysis of data from previous periods of activity?

Source: Authors' own study based on: https://logisticaudit.wordpress.com/

indicators. At the same time, what should be emphasized here is that – in narrow terms – the analysis of performance, additionally includes:

- bottleneck analysis, which consists of identifying constraints and then minimizing or eliminating them, in order to improve the efficiency of processes taking place in the logistics system and subsystems of the organization,
- processing times analysis, which is associated with the assessment of the actual state of the order processing-time with the time of stay (the period in which a given item or service stayed in the selected area),
- deadline task analysis, which includes the assessment of the summary of the implementation of specific tasks in terms of defined deadlines. In practice, this type of analysis gives the opportunity to obtain a relatively objective picture related to the generation of additional costs, resulting from exceeding the time of task implementation in selected subsystems of the logistics system,
- error analysis, which consists of documenting (recording) errors that may occur both in relation to the objects being subjected to measurement, may be dictated by the properties of the measurement tool, or may be related to the bias of the person making the measurement. In addition, it is worth adding here that errors in the functioning of the logistics system can be characterized by regularity, randomness, but also excessiveness. A thorough analysis of these errors, however, allows for a precise estimation of the costs they generate in the organization's logistics system,
- cost logistic analysis, which provides information on the location, level, and dynamics of cost formation in various areas and subsystems of the logistics system. Thanks to the information obtained in

this area, the enterprise management can initiate actions aimed at reducing costs, e.g., by launching cost-reduction programs.

- in the third stage – process analysis provides a series of activities whose main goal is to gain understanding in the functioning of all logistics processes taking place in the logistics system of the organization. Knowledge about processes is obtained mainly from reviewing the elements of the process, getting acquainted with its input and output data, checking procedures and control systems, evaluating the applications used, or interacting with other objects and devices. Therefore, when making a holistic assessment of the potential of a given process in a logistics system, the following are taken into account: master data (including data on technological solutions, suppliers, customers, products, services, contracts, locations), time, costs, warehouse inventory, quality and continuous improvement policy, internal and external work organization, process planning and control policy, material and intangible resources of the organization, methods supply-chain management, the possibility of using the "make or buy" method (see Table 4.2),
- in the fourth stage – structure analysis provides the opportunity to assess the existing system structure, from the point of view of the conditions in which it operates. The subject of the analysis of the structure of an object or system may be its level: flexibility, complexity, modernity, centralization, hierarchy, network of connections, and interdependencies, etc.,
- in the fifth stage – comparative analysis allows the identification of differences and similarities occurring in the company's logistics system compared to others on the market. This type of analysis can be carried out using, for example, the benchmarking method.

The above-outlined five-step procedure for analyzing the potential of the logistics system (see: Figure 4.4) enriches the role of the logistics audit in improving the enterprise in general and the logistics system in particular. In addition, it is a comprehensive tool in identifying and removing barriers in the subsystems of the logistics system that limit its ability to implement the process of continuous improvement. In addition, the presented procedure clearly changes the essence of the logistics audit approach to the challenges and problems it faces, from reactive to proactive. As Nogalski and Marcinkiewicz (2004) argue, such an attitude may even be a starting point for the development of a model of proactive and reactive actions, which will be a recipe for crisis situations that the enterprise may face in the future. Therefore, let us note that the scale of the impact of a logistics audit on the organization may, as is often the case, take on a strategic character.

4.3. Logistics audit in the organization – identification of risks in logistics processes

The implementation of a logistics audit in the organization, *ex definitione*, provides it with information both about the possibilities and directions of improving the current situation in which it is located as well as the processes that are implemented in its logistics system. In practice, the auditor, in order to acquire knowledge – especially in the area of logistics processes – subjects an organization to a thorough analysis in terms of quality, efficiency, technology used, the impact of exogenous factors, or susceptibility to changes and the occurrence of crisis situations. However, one of the overarching goals that guide the implementation of a logistics audit is to identify potential threats and risks[9] that may occur within logistics processes. Recognition should be understood not only as the identification of risks, their measurement, or giving them a hierarchy of "importance," but also their quantitative and qualitative estimation, taking into account also – and perhaps above all – the probability of occurrence of a given phenomenon or situation in the future. However, before we move on to the description of the types of risks and issues related to them in the context of logistics processes and logistics audit, let's first refer to the essence and definition of the concept of risk. As noted by Buła (2015b), risk is an interdisciplinary category that can be considered in psychological-sociological, mathematical-statistical, and financial terms. Nevertheless, it is in the social sciences (and especially in economics) that it is the subject of the most numerous applications, approaches, or studies. But, paradoxically, the multifaceted nature of the term determines its complexity, which is emphasized mainly by the number of scientific interpretations and approaches. What's more, one can even put forward the thesis that risk, as a phenomenon, is one of the better described conceptual categories in modern management science, which – despite the passage of time and its popularity – still has the potential for research and scientific development. In dictionary terms, the term "risk," which derives from the Dutch *risico*, or German *risiko*, means an action with unknown effects. As a non-objective category in management science, risk refers mainly to economic, financial, and organizational projects, the result of which is unknown, uncertain, or unpredictable in any way, without the use of the measurement techniques available today. Risk is, which should be clearly emphasized here, a chronic phenomenon, an element that constantly accompanies the organization (see Figure 4.3) and is present in it, at various levels of the organizational structure. In addition, it is a category whose sources of origin can be diverse and multifaceted, which in tabular terms is presented in Table 4.3.

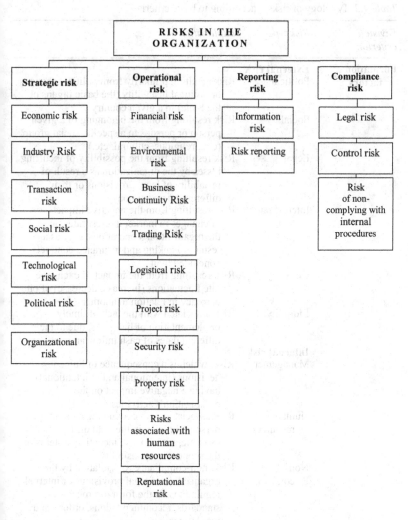

Figure 4.3 Categories and types of risks in the organization Source: Authors' own study based on Bekefi et al. 2008, p. 10.

Thus, it should be stated that the risk always exists, it results from something and something accompanies, increases, or decreases it, and it is an immanent feature of the functioning of any organization. However, if we wanted to define risk in the context of logistics systems, Szymonik (2014) argues that risk is the conditions under which the logistician knows the likelihood of an activity being obtained by a deliberately organized and

Table 4.3 Typology of risks – according to basic criteria

Division criterion	Risk type	Explanation
Formation factors	**External risk**	
	Political	Risk resulting primarily from political changes or political instability (the basic organs of the State) in a given country
	Social	Risk resulting from the belonging of a given person or persons to a specific social group (e.g., religious, cultural, etc.)
	Legal	Risk resulting from the possibility of incurring losses by the organization as a result of instability of legal provisions or their different interpretations
	Interest rate	Risk resulting from the negative impact of changes in market interest rates on the organization's operations, e.g., as a result of banking and insurance contracts concluded by it
	Currency	Risk resulting from the impact of exchange rate fluctuations (increase, decrease) of one currency in relation to another
	Liquidity	Risk associated with the lack of timely implementation of liabilities, due to the different dates of cash inflow and outflow
	Internal risk	
	Management	Risk, which is a consequence of human decisions (intentional and unintentional), having a negative impact on the organization's activities
	Human resources	Risk associated with conducting an improper personnel policy in the field of, for example, recruitment, incentive systems or the scope of responsibility
	Non-compliance	Risk, non-compliance, or violation by the organization of legal provisions or internal regulations, in the form of procedures, standards, recommendations, orders, and regulations
	Corporate	Risk that refers to the obligations and threats facing the organization, related to, for example, IT failures
Repeatability	Systematic	Risk that is caused by general economic factors, most often of a global nature, over which organizations have no influence because they are shaped in a way that is independent of their will or actions taken

(Continued)

Table 4.3 (Continued)

Division criterion	Risk type	Explanation
	Specific	Risk that is individual and is associated with a specific business activity of a person or organization. Its source may be, for example, competition or a specific type of investment
Effect	Pure	Risk that occurs when there is a danger of incurring a loss, without any chance of winning. Most often, this type of risk concerns events of a random nature
	Speculative	Risk that can cause both losses and profits. This is a risk that is taken consciously
Time	Strategic	Long-term risk related to the existence of the organization
	Operating	Short-term risk related to the current functioning of the organization
Variability of the environment	Static	Risk, occurring constantly regardless of technical or economic progress, associated with the occurrence of the forces of nature
	Dynamic	Risk that occurs in connection with continuous technological, economic, economic, and social progress
Impact measurement	Financial	Risk whose impact can be quantified and assessed from the point of view of the financial results of the organization
	Non-financial	Risk whose impact cannot be quantified and assessed from the point of view of the organization's financial results

Source: Authors' own study based on: Młodzik, 2013, pp. 441–442.

combined set of elements (subsystems) such as procurement, production, distribution, together with the relationships between them and their properties conditioning the flow of material and information. Therefore, we can see that, in synthetic terms, the risk in the logistics system is the sum of adverse phenomena or events occurring in the subsystems that make it up, including transport, procurement, storage, production, order fulfillment, distribution, and supply chain. With this in mind, including the topic of this section, we will now move on to defining risks in relation to logistics processes. We will determine the state characterized by the uncertainty of the occurrence of undesirable events in the integrated – in terms of time, costs, and goals – flow of tangible and intangible resources in the organization's business activity, aimed at satisfying the needs of customers. Kuklińska and Koziarska (2017) emphasize that risk in logistics processes appears regardless of the size of the enterprise, its organizational and legal form, the sector or industry in which it operates, as well as its position on the market. Nevertheless, its scope, impact, or frequency of occurrence is largely determined by the prism of the appearance of modern logistic processes, which are characterized by greater dynamics, complexity, or length, as well as susceptibility to endogenous and exogenous factors. Due to the fact that phenomena with unknown effects (read: risks) are gaining strength in logistics processes – both in quantitative and qualitative terms – the role (prestige) of the logistics audit as the tool for their identification and elimination, is also increasing. And although this is not an easy task, a logistics audit can serve as an effective tool in identifying categories, types, or groups of risks occurring in logistics processes. Their numbers and multifaceted nature are presented in Table 4.4.

The above-presented in table 4.3 categories, types, and groups of risks to which enterprises are exposed, as are their logistic systems and processes functioning within them, do not exhaust either their long list or the entire problem that is related to this phenomenon. From the point of view of the enterprise and the elements that make up it, selected risks may disappear (or weaken), and in their place may arise new ones related to the development of the digital economy[10] and, consequently, to digital risk. In practice, enterprises – taking into account the wide spectrum of activities and tasks carried out – should therefore create their own list of risks that are important and critical for their functioning and the business environment. Then, such a risk register should be the subject of the logistics audit, which will examine, assess, and indicate the possibility of adverse events, especially in the area of the organization's logistics system, and recommend a way to eliminate or reduce them.

4.4. The impact of digitalization on the logistics audit

Digitalization is one of the most important megatrends in the world, along with growing migratory flows, the development of a circular economy, cultural convergence, and growing inequalities, or the flourishing of integrated mobility and global supply chains. In practice, the changes it causes (that are often dynamic, but also groundbreaking) with their scope and scale of impact cover both the poor and the rich, developed, and developing countries,[11] as well as all societies and organizations. In view of this, it is not surprising that digitalization is a leading topic of many global events and is the epicenter of scientific interest among researchers and experts. But the important thing is that we are currently only at the beginning of its development. This situation determines several discrepancies and the lack of commonly accepted definitions in science as to terms related not only to digitalization itself, but also to

Table 4.4 Groups of risk in logistics processes

Type of process	Type of logistics processes	Risk groups
Basic processes	Execution of orders (orders) of the client	• Failure to meet the delivery time • Decrease in the number of orders • Defect in the execution of the order
	Implementation of logistic customer service	• Underdevelopment of solutions • Hardware failure • Lack of experience
	Offering additional value to the customer	• Changes in the values offered
	Minimization of costs leading to a reduction in the price of the product and service offer	• Deterioration of quality • Loss of some elite customers
	Receiving and shipping products through the processes of transport, handling, storage, packaging, and marking of products	• Failure to meet the lead time • Decrease in the number of orders • Lack of integration between production, distribution, and transport processes
	Providing the required level of logistical customer service	• Inadequate level of services provided • Insufficiently customer-oriented service process, non-performance of contracts by carriers, logistics operators, etc. • Failure of suppliers to comply with technical standards • Quality control system of materials • Punctuality of deliveries
Supporting processes	Analysis and forecast of market logistics situations	• Faulty logistic information system
	Identification of customer preferences and expectations in the field of logistics service	• Problem with identifying key customers or groups of buyers • Inaccurate prediction of customer needs
	Identification of logistic market segments	• Failure to adapt the offer of logistics services to the segment • Lack of integration of all activities related to a given logistics segment
	Development and development of logistics strategies	• Failure to adapt the offer of logistics services to the segment • Lack of integration of all activities related to a given logistics segment
	Development of the set and structure of logistics components mix	• Service-level decisions • Planning of material requirements • Placing orders • Supply forecasting • Location of warehouses and warehouses

(*Continued*)

Table 4.4 (Continued)

Type of process	Type of logistics processes	Risk groups
	Securing and developing the qualifications of personnel in the field of competence in the design and implementation of logistics processes	• Poor production planning
	Securing the quality of service delivery processes	• Inadequate level of services provided
	Securing the quality of product purchase and sale processes	• Incorrect assessment of the quality of materials • Supplier rating error • Incorrect selection of suppliers • Faulty quality control assessment of finished products
	Control the flow of products by developing the processes of transport, handling, storage, packaging, and marking of goods	• Lack of internal and external integration in supply chain management
	Issuing instructions regarding the execution of orders and customer orders	• Excessively long time to provide information • Unreadability of information • Misinterpretation of commands
	Identification of goals and development of assumptions for the implementation of logistic customer service	• Inadequate ability of partners to respond to unexpected orders (low flexibility, too-slow adaptation to requirements)
Tertiary processes	Securing capacities and potentials for creating added value	• Lack of innovative solutions • Lack of implementation of strategies, plans in practice • Limiting oneself to proclaiming slogans (lack of implementation) • The impact of promotion and advertising
	Research and development of logistics infrastructure	• Changes in delivery conditions • Poor production planning • Lack of flexibility in the production process
	Development of information and information technology	• Lack or insufficient flow of information about demand from points of sale and from key customers • Inadequate methods of demand forecasting, problems in the flow of information
	Shaping and maintaining relations and relations with the environment	• Imbalance between customer expectations and the capabilities of all links of the supply chain, misunderstanding of market needs

(Continued)

Table 4.4 (Continued)

Type of process	Type of logistics processes	Risk groups
	Management of waste, packaging, permanently damaged products	• Lack of integration with customers • Volatility of demand, relations with contractors • Competitive forces on the market • Market potential • No regulation of waste recirculation • Insufficient environmental awareness • No hazardous waste collection system • No landfills that meet legal requirements • No separate collection of waste
	Securing sales and turnover	• Errors in planning material requirements • Having unnecessary supplies
	Securing the financial aspects of logistics (execution of customer accounts)	• Errors in estimating the customer's profitability • Too-high service costs • Volatility of material prices • Underestimation of projected costs

Source: (Lwowski & Kozłowski, 2007, p. 126).

its close words, such as *digitization* or *digital transformation.* Their source can be both the constant perception of *digitization* in terms of neologisms, as well as ambiguities related to its phenomenon itself. With this in mind, it can be concluded that technology not only changes the language but also often overtakes it. In order to explain how the phenomenon of digitization will affect the implementation of a logistics audit (or audit in general) in an enterprise, we must here – for the sake of clarity of argument and terminological order – define three basic concepts: digitization, digitalization, and digital transformation (see Table 4.5). Apart from the wealth of definitions available in literature, in general terms, digitalization can be understood as a digital (virtual) form of reality. In dictionary terms, digitalization is about using digital technologies to change the existing business model in an organization and provide it with new opportunities to generate revenue and value. The main goal of digitalization is the complete automation of existing operations and business processes of the enterprise. A term close – albeit unequal – to the concept of digitalization is digitization. Łobejko (2018) defines digitization as the process of giving information a digital form. The main goal of digitization, which in fact gave rise to digitization, is to change the document format from analog (not related to computer technology) to digital. Note, then, that what distinguishes the two is that digitization is a "higher" form of digitalization. The only similarity that exists between these concepts is that both digitization and digitalization are processes (systems of successive causally related changes); however, where digitalization should be combined with the process of improvement, digitization should be combined with the process of transformation. The final element of this development process, at the base of which is digitization and at a higher level, digitalization, is digital transformation. In the definition presented by Mazzone (2014), digital transformation is an evolutionary process of a permanent and purposeful nature, which takes place in an organization, which is aimed at its complete digitization (see Table 4.5). This means that digital transformation in the enterprise is subject to the business model, processes,

Table 4.5 Digitalization, digitization, digital transformation – a comparative approach

	Digitalization	*Digitization*	*Digital Transformation*
Beginnings of development	1950s	1970s	2000s
Applies to	Data conversion	Data processing	Use of knowledge
Purpose	Changing the format from analog to digital	Automation of existing operations and business processes	Changing the organizational culture of the company and the ways in which it acts and thinks
Activity	Convert paper documents, photos, microfilms, LPs*, films and VHS tapes** to digital format	Creating digital work processes	Creating a new digital organization
Tools	Computers and tools for conversion and encoding	IT systems and computer applications	Matrix of new (breakthrough) digital technologies
Challenge	Volume, material	Price, financing	Resistance to changes in human resources
Examples	Scanning of paper registration forms	Electronic registration process	Everything electronic from registration forms to delivered content

Source: Authors' own study based on Savić, 2019, p. 37.
* LP (long play) – vinyl, long playing records. ** VHS (video home system) – a standard for recording video cassettes.

procedures, management methods, as well as relations with customers or employees of the organization. The result of these activities is the creation of a new, digital organization. At this point, however, it should be noted that digital transformation is a serious leadership challenge for those who lead and oversee it. The point is that this type of transformation is aimed at reviving the organization and radically improving its efficiency. The materialization of these aspirations, however, is possible thanks to the skillful use of the potential that lies dormant in global digital technology.

The key factors driving the development of digitization[12] (see Figure 4.4), and thus the creation of the digital economy[13,14] (or *cyber economy*) include primarily (Pieriegud, 2016):

- the Internet of Things, the Internet of Services, and the Internet of Everything,[15]

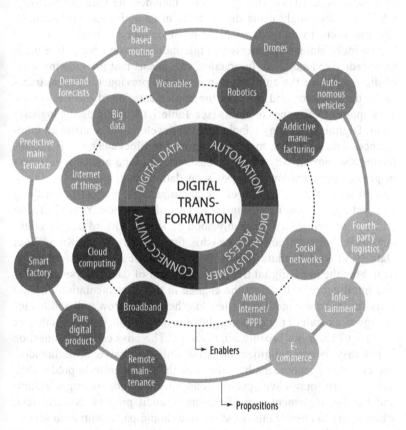

Figure 4.4 Drivers of digitization Source: (Roland Berger, 2015, p. 20).

- ubiquitous connectivity,
- applications and services based on cloud computing,
- big-data analytics and big data as a service,
- automation and robotization,
- multi-channel and omni-channel distribution models of products and services,
- global supply chains.

The consequence of the fact that for nearly two decades the phenomenon of digitization has been accompanying and co-determining the economic development of the world is that some industries have already reached the status of digital maturity. Among them, the most frequently mentioned are telecommunications, technology, media and entertainment, automotive, financial, banking, insurance, manufacturing, or retail trade (Adamczewski, 2018). This group also includes the logistics industry, which is increasingly using digital tools in its activities. For example, one can point to methods of planning inventory volumes, which are increasingly being implemented in this industry using predictive models (predictive analytics). In practice, this means that the growing level of digitization of the enterprise, in a manner previously unseen, transforms the image of, and tools for, the implementation of audit activities. This applies to all types of audits (see Table 1.1), including the logistics audit. Digital technology – including the development of artificial intelligence, data analytics, machine learning, or blockchain[16] – is recomposing the current way of doing business and data analysis, resulting in greater organizational emphasis on data management. From this it also follows that the burden of the organization's interest in verifying and getting to know its customers as part of the Know Your Customer (KYC)[17] procedure will probably soon be shifted toward deeper familiarization, but with current data, this time as part of the Know Your Data (KYD)[18] procedure (Khan, 2018). The question therefore arises as to how the main digital trends (in the form of data analysis or artificial intelligence) will affect the change in the implementation of audit activities and their methodologies. In other words, how will audits face change as a result of the growing global pressure from digital trends (see Table 4.6) or, more broadly, digitization. The answer to this question is not easy, because digitization is not only a massive, multithreaded, and complex phenomenon but, also, one that is not entirely predictable. This, in turn, may have specific consequences both for organizations and for the implementation of the entire audit process. Nevertheless, when trying to answer this question, one should pay attention to several

Table 4.6 Strategic technological trends of the 21st century

Trend	The name of the technological trend	Trend characteristics
Trend 1	Internet of Behaviors (IoB)	In the case of commercial vehicles, behavioral Internet technology can be used in the telematics of transport systems to monitor the behavior of drivers while driving, related to, e.g., sudden braking or making an aggressive turn. Then, the data collected in this way can be used by organizations to improve the efficiency of drivers' working time through better route planning and overall safety improvements. However, this technology can also be used by insurance institutions, especially those who want to monitor the level of physical activity of the insured person, in order to determine their contributions, in the context of their life insurance policy. And such practices can already cause serious ethical or social consequences
Trend 2	Total experience	Holistic experience is the sum of the experiences of all customers, employees, suppliers, users, etc., which is aimed at changing the result of business activity. Its goal is to improve the overall experience in the place where all these elements intersect. Linking all these experiences (as opposed to an individual approach) can serve an organization to differentiate itself from its competitors in a way that is difficult to reproduce, which will be reflected in building a more lasting competitive advantage
Trend 3	Privacy-enhancing computation	Privacy computing is three technologies designed to protect your data as it is used. The first provides a trusted environment in which sensitive data is processed. The second analyzes data in a decentralized manner. And the third encrypts data and algorithms before processing or analyzing them. In practice, this technology allows organizations to securely collaborate in different "configurations" without sacrificing their confidentiality and privacy
Trend 4	Distributed cloud	A distributed cloud (an integrated, multi-cloud world) is a place where cloud services are distributed to various physical locations, with the public cloud provider being responsible for and supervising it. The distributed cloud is considered the future of the cloud services market, due to the fact that the use of a public cloud is cheaper and less complex than in the case of a private cloud. In addition, private clouds are gradually becoming an equal partner for public clouds

(Continued)

Table 4.6 (Continued)

Trend	The name of the technological trend	Trend characteristics
Trend 5	Anywhere operations	A technology and operating model that will enable you to work from anywhere and improve the implementation of business services in a distributed IT infrastructure. Thanks to this solution, owners, employees, customers, or business partners will be able to cooperate and operate physically in remote environments. It is, in other words, a digital enhancement of physical space
Trend 6	Cybersecurity mesh	Cybersecurity mesh is a distributed architectural approach that aims to create a scalable security mechanism that can be quickly adapted to the necessary level of security. As a rule, a cybersecurity network allows users to define a security boundary around the identity of a person or a specific thing
Trend 7	Intelligent composable business	A smart business that is composable is one that can be modified and quickly changed depending on the situation. In practice, digital transformation forces organizations to compose structures, models, and business strategies that will be flexible and have the ability to quickly adapt to changing conditions
Trend 8	AI engineering	A robust AI engineering strategy will facilitate the performance, scalability, interpretability, and reliability of AI models while delivering the full value of your AI investment. It is not uncommon for projects related to artificial intelligence technology to encounter problems in organizations related to their profitability, durability, and management
Trend 9	Hyperautoma-tion	Hyperautomation is a process that involves automating as many business or IT processes as possible, using highly advanced digital tools in the form of artificial intelligence, machine learning, etc. Indirectly, it is driven by those organizations that have older business processes and which (due to changing conditions) need improvement, especially since the efficiency, effectiveness, and business flexibility of processes today determine the market position of many organizations
Trend 10	Blockchain	Blockchain is a blockchain technology (information arranged in blocks) that can be public or private. It is currently a new way of documenting data on the Internet. In practice, it is used to create blockchain applications, such as predictive markets, games, storage platforms, social networks, online stores, etc.

Source: Authors' own study based on Burke, 2020.

important threads and interdependencies between the development of digitization and auditing (including the logistics audit):

- first, the functions that a modern audit has to perform should keep up with the changes that emerge in the area of digital technology. This means that all processes, procedures, and practices carried out as part of audit activities, based on digital technology, must comply with the legal, ethical, and social requirements in the enterprise,

- second, the increase in the number of intelligent organizations forces audit methodologies to seek out and invest in new digital technologies in order to meet the challenges from customers related to the audit service, especially in the area of data analysis,

- third, the rapid growth of data (information) from various sources in organizations, including systems, sensors, databases, or cameras, offers the possibility of conducting a more efficient audit, with higher quality and greater added value for the organization. This is because the new digital tools used in audit – in the form of automated analytical algorithms – provide an opportunity to test entire sets of structured data held by the organization and not, as previously, only its selected, representative samples. Thus, in practice, they eliminate the need to conduct additional audits in the event of unexpected errors,

- fourth, the development of cloud computing[19] technology means that organizations are increasingly processing and storing their data in the cloud. However, access to cloud resources is available not only to employees of the organization but also to third parties. As a consequence, solutions based on cloud computing require auditors to include in their audit tasks additional activities related to the verification of access and functions performed in the context of cybersecurity,

- fifth, companies that currently want to keep up with the dynamically developing and changing organizational environment are beginning, more and more often, to use the knowledge derived from the analysis of large data sets (big data). And although the volume (quantity), velocity, variety, veracity (credibility), as well as the value[20] of these data sets is difficult to process and interpret, they are, at the same time, a valuable source of acquisition of new resources of knowledge about the organization and its environment.[21] However, from the point of view of auditing, the identification and analysis of large data sets can serve as another tool supporting the risk-assessment process in the organization,

- sixth, the growing prevalence of digital tools will foster the dynamic development of remote audits, which can be performed from anywhere in the world and will not require the physical presence of an auditor in the organization (parent or client). In addition, audit activities, such as the review of documents or interviews, will increasingly be carried out in real time, using the most modern ICT solutions,

- seventh, the ongoing changes will force organizations providing internal audit services (including industry audits) and external audit to find a quick answer to the question of how to audit innovative technologies, whether in the form of intelligent machines, robots, or processes, while taking into account audit quality, the time and costs of its implementation, and applicable laws (Meuldijk, 2017),

- eighth, digitization will necessitate the development of digital skills. A key role in this process will be played by both sectoral schools and universities,[22] which must ensure that this type of qualification is developed among societies. Thus, those education systems that have so far considered thematic areas such as cybernetics or algorithmics as niche, will become outdated. Digital competences, in particular, will be required in the audit profession, both in terms of expertise in auditing intelligent systems, processes, or entire enterprises, as well as the rapid development of remote audits,

- ninth, the evolution of digital technologies will undermine the current value of audit services. So far, the costs of the audit have been largely dependent on the time required for its implementation, but now, thanks to technology, it will be significantly shortened, and thus the fees for audit services will be based primarily on knowledge, support, and the ability to combine them with the enterprise's strategy. In other words, a good audit and its value will depend in the future on the ability to anticipate changes so that the customer can be offered appropriate recommendations and support services,

- tenth, organizations (individuals) providing audit services (including industry audits, including the logistics audit) must invest in the recruitment of digital talent, in cooperation with experts and specialists in the field of digitization and digitization, in artificial intelligence technology and blockchain, in big-data analytics, and cybersecurity. Only then will they be able to deal with the potential challenges and threats that their customers, business partners, or stakeholders will also face.

Finally, it should be noted that the pace and strength of impact from new digital technologies on the audit area (see Figure 4.5) is – in the history of its development – unprecedented and multifaceted. Therefore, in the coming decades, Audit 4.0 will strongly evolve toward the development of Audit 5.0, which will be not only computerized but, above all, remote and digital (see Figures 1.2 and 4.5). In addition, its current reputation – developed

Figure 4.5 Trends determining the development of Audit 5.0 Source: Authors' own study.

over recent years – will require revitalization, due to the fact that the audit will have to face a postmodern reality that will be unprecedented in terms of challenges and changes.

Thus, how the audit will cope with the new digital reality will in the future determine its market position and the value it will represent for enterprises. This task will not be easy, because the audit will have to deal with issues such as digital transformation, investments in new digital technologies, recruitment of people with digital skills, remodeling of existing ways of carrying out audit activities, adaptation to the requirements of digital law (digital rights), launching new forms of communication with stakeholders, and generating business insights anticipating future, possible events (also in relation to various types of risks).

4.5.   The current Polish and European market for logistics audit services

The logistics services market in Poland began to develop at the beginning of the 1990s, which was a direct consequence of changes related to its economic and political transformation. In practice, this was reflected in the fact that the centrally planned economy ceased to exist, and in its place a free market and economic freedom were created. These circumstances, with the systematically growing involvement of foreign capital in Poland (in the form of foreign direct investment (FDI) inflow – see Figure 4.6), led to an increase in aggregate demand and the gradual development of the transport, shipping, and logistics (TSL) sector.

Currently, the logistics industry is one of the most important branches of the Polish economy, which in terms of size also stands out among European nations. Despite the global COVID-19 pandemic, further prospects for its development are also promising and the dynamics of economic growth in Poland, even in the situation of its slowdown in Western European countries, will continue to be stimulated even in 2023 through (PwC, 2019):

- a large and absorbent internal market and the further enrichment of society, which in practice will contribute to an increase in consumer demand,

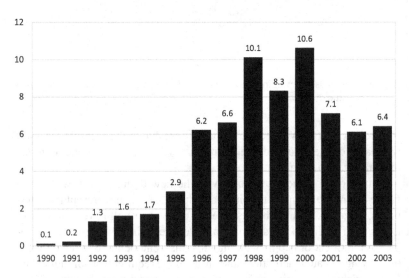

Figure 4.6 Inflow of foreign direct investment into Poland, 1990–2003 (in USD billion) Source: Authors' own study based on Polish Investment and Trade Agency.

- further inflows of EU funds, which will stimulate the level of national investment,
- continued lower labor costs compared to Western European countries (including Germany, France, Belgium, or the Netherlands),
- attractive location of Poland, which therefore draws in foreign investments in industrial plants and distribution centers,
- a well-organized institutional system, especially compared to other countries in Central and Eastern Europe.

Nevertheless, a possible slowdown in economic growth in the rest of Europe should not have a significant impact on the European logistics market, which, according to specialists, is expected to increase by an additional USD 217 billion during 2020–2024.[23] The source of such optimistic forecasts for the logistics industry – despite the COVID-19 pandemic – is the growing number of mergers and acquisitions across the world and a significant increase in global demand in e-commerce, which is expected to reach more than USD 6.5 trillion by 2023. If these forecasts are confirmed, it will mean that in just one decade the level of e-commerce sales on a global scale has increased by over 610% (see Figure 4.7).

Optimistic scenarios for the development of the logistics services market in Poland and Europe, however, should not obscure the challenges faced by

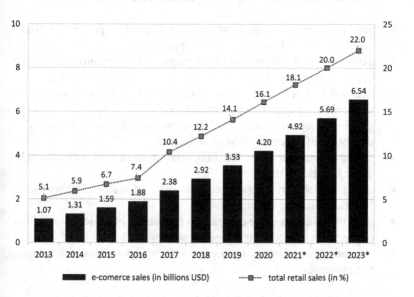

Figure 4.7 Global level of e-commerce sales, 2013–2023 forecast Source: Own study based on eMarketer, Dec 2014 and May 2019.

the industry in the light of the transformation taking place today. It is primarily about the geometrically advancing digitization and the lack of people on the labor market with specific competences, especially given that, in the next two to three years, technologies such as artificial intelligence, IoT, big data, or DLT[24] technology will reach maturity, allowing for a wider use of software (applications), not only in logistics, but also in many other industries (PwC, 2019). In view of the above, it should therefore be expected that, with the further development of the logistics services sector, there will also be a proportional increase in the demand for logistics audit services. In order to improve their efficiency and competitiveness, enterprises will be forced by digital transformation to remodel their existing activities, strategies, and management methods. In this situation, the logistics audit, as a consulting service, can become an indispensable support tool, not only in the context of assessing the state of logistics and improving the functioning of enterprise logistics system but also in the transformation of the current business model into a more "pro-digital" one. In other words, a logistics audit may be necessary to eliminate the organizational dysfunctions of a given enterprise and help to optimize its business strategy; all the more so because, in fact, it is related to the logistics strategy, which in turn is related to the logistics audit.

Nevertheless, current global megatrends alone do not affect the need to decide to conduct a logistics audit in the organization. In practice, the desire to implement such an audit can be triggered by other forces:

- need to improve management activities focused on production, warehousing, transport, distribution, or supply chain,
- assessment of the degree of competitiveness of the organization against the market, in order to implement an effective management strategy,
- decrease in the efficiency of the functioning of certain subsystems such as the logistics system of the organization,
- growing problems in the scalability of business, due to issues related to the costs and expenses of the organization,
- increasing number of errors, difficulties, dysfunctions, or bottlenecks in the logistics system,
- desire to make an independent assessment of the functioning of the logistics system in the organization,
- need for valuation of the company in the context of the implementation of processes related to its merger or acquisition,
- reorganization of internal processes and implementation of new logistics processes.

The management team's decision to carry out a logistics audit in the enterprise entails the need to take another decision related to the form in which it will be carried out. In this case, the issue is whether the logistics audit will be carried out using the internal resources of the enterprise or with the participation of an external entity. The consequence of choosing the second option is that it carries certain risks related to, for example, access by third parties to the company's information, which may be characterized by different levels of sensitivity. Therefore, in order to limit these risks, it is necessary to make a market-based decision regarding the selection of a logistics audit provider, which will take into account issues related to:

- first, comprehensiveness of the audit conducted by the auditor, taking into account and analyzing the cause-and-effect activities (a small change in one subsystem of the company's logistics system may affect both its other elements and the entire system),
- second, the qualifications, experience, and references possessed by the auditor(s), which should coincide with the problem areas occurring in the organization commissioning the audit,
- third, customization of services provided, which will not be of a mass nature but will be tailored to the specific needs and requirements of customers commissioning the implementation of logistics audit services,
- fourth, costs of conducting a logistic audit together with other conditions contained in the commercial contract for its realization.

Bearing in mind the above, we can see that the process of selecting an external entity providing logistics audit services to a given enterprise is not a simple task. It often has a multi-stage character and is subject to various analyses, which ultimately should offer confidence to enterprise management about the correctness of the choice made. Nowadays, on the Polish and European markets, there are various enterprises or institutes that specialize in conducting logistics audits for both private and public business entities (see Table 4.7). Their number is increasing year on year.

On the one hand, this growth is due to the development of logistics and the logistics services market itself, which, in practice, leads to an increase in the number of entities operating within it; and, on the other hand, to the growing demand for audit and logistics consulting services. It should be noted that the entities operating on the market, in addition to logistics audit services, also offer other services in the form of logistics consulting, design of logistics systems, automation of logistics processes (including storage, production, distribution, or supply-chain processes), implementation of e-logistics solutions, and design of logistics systems based on artificial intelligence. Nevertheless, it is the logistics audit that is the service that is most often chosen by enterprises and implemented in various areas of the logistics system. As a result, the following are commonly debated

Table 4.7 Polish providers of consultancy services in logistics audit

Enterprise	Scope of activity
OPTIDATA	The company was founded in 2002, specializing in providing comprehensive solutions for production logistics. This barcode systems or RFID technology supporting production, warehouse, and transport processes. It provides logistics audit services in areas related mainly to storage, production, and transport. It employs people specializing in WMS* and TMS** systems
CHAINGERS	The company was founded in 2005, and is one of the leaders on the Polish market in the field of logistics consulting. It specializes in providing services in the field of logistics audit (in the areas of production, warehousing, supply chain, distribution network, logistics system, and enterprise), logistics strategies, process automation, logistics optimization, warehouse design, and logistics project management. The company's offer is used by the following industries: construction, FMCG***, automotive, electrotechnical, chemical, pharmaceutical, printing, production, tourism, advertising, logistics, and forwarding
ASPECT	Founded in 2002, the company is engaged in the analysis and optimization of the logistics infrastructure of the organization. It provides logistics audit services in the areas of storage, production, and distribution networks. It specializes in the implementation of quick controls. The company's offer is used by the following industries: footwear, forwarding, household appliances/electronics, and furniture
LOGIFACT LOGISTICS SYSTEMS	The beginnings of the company date back to 1999. Since its inception, it has been focused on the design and implementation of WMS. In addition, it is focused on supporting warehouse logistics at the level of operational management. Its portfolio includes over 150 implementations of WMS systems, on both the Polish and the international markets. The company's offer in the field of consulting services includes logistics consulting, logistics optimization for the warehouse management area, and logistics audit
ELANDIS	Founded in Krakow in 2012, the company, from the beginning of its activity, has focused on providing consulting and design services in the area of the supply chain. It provides services in the field of logistics audit of production, warehouse, and distribution. Through its dynamic development and professionalism in the provision of services, the company aspires to the role of an authority in the field of logistics consulting services on the domestic and foreign markets

(Continued)

Table 4.7 (Continued)

Enterprise	Scope of activity
ŁUKASIEWICZ RESEARCH NETWORK – INSTITUTE OF LOGISTICS AND WAREHOUSING	The Network is a market-oriented research and development unit, performing the functions of the Polish competence center in logistics and e-economy. The Institute was founded in 1967 and since 1 April 2019 has been part of the Łukasiewicz Research Network. In addition to conducting research, the institute also provides services to external private entities in the field of audit of logistics processes

Source: Authors' own study.
*WMS – warehouse management systems. **TMS – transportation management system.
***FMCG – fast moving consumer goods.

procedures: logistics audit of procurement, logistics audit of the warehouse, logistics audit of production, logistics audit of distribution, logistics audit of the supply chain, etc. Finally, it should be emphasized that a competently conducted logistics audit will be an important element of support for the enterprise, primarily by assessing the extent to which its logistics system achieves economic efficiency, effectiveness, and economy.

4.6. Control and analytical questions

Control questions

1. Detail the four tasks on which the logistics audit focuses as part of the overall assessment of the logistics system.
2. What is the performance analysis in the five-stage assessment of the potential of the enterprise's logistics system?
3. Present the types and types of risks that occur in the enterprise.
4. Define the risks that occur in basic logistics processes.
5. Provide a definition of digitization and digitization, and then determine the difference between these conceptual categories.
6. Identify the key drivers of digitalization.
7. What do the acronyms KYC and KYD mean?
8. What is hyperautomation?
9. Name the five trends that determine the development of Audit 5.0.
10. What factors can influence the development of the logistics audit services market in Poland?

Analytical questions

1. Is it right that audit is considered a tool for improving the enterprise? If so, why? What other management instruments do you think

can be subject to the improvement process as part of the functioning of the enterprise?

2. List and briefly characterize the groups of risks occurring in logistics processes, divided into basic, supporting, and tertiary processes.

3. In your opinion, how do the phenomena of digitization, digitalization, and digital transformation affect the development and implementation of the audit? Identify the benefits and risks of these processes for an enterprise.

4. How will hyperautomation and artificial intelligence affect the further development of auditing, including the logistics audit? How will Audit 5.0 (fifth generation) differ from Audit 4.0 (fourth generation)?

5. How do you assess the prospects for the development of the logistics consulting services market, including logistics audit, in Poland? Taking into account the importance of the logistics sector for the Polish economy, do you think that Poland has a chance to become a leader in the provision of logistics audit services in Europe?

Notes

1 Meanwhile, an organization's pursuit of excellence can also be dangerous, especially in situations where management is constantly striving to achieve unrealistic goals and building a dangerous sense among employees that higher-level values in the organization are only perceived in terms of productivity, efficiency, and purposefulness.

2 A model developed by the global consulting firm McKinsey & Company, where the acronym 7S stands for: strategy, systems, structure, shared values, skills, styles, staff.

3 These are products, in the form of a material object, a plan, technology, or language, which are the work of the human mind and human labor.

4 For more on this, see Testa and Sipe, 2013.

5 It was established at the end of the 19th and the beginning of the 20th centuries.

6 The word "analysis" comes from the Greek word *anàlysis*, meaning "disassembly into parts."

7 For more on this topic, see Twaróg, 2003.

8 See: https://logisticaudit.wordpress.com/

9 Extremely often, especially in everyday speech and journalistic writing, the words "threat" and "risk" are treated as if they are synonymous. Meanwhile, threat is something potentially harmful, while risk is, in fact, the probability of a harmful hazard occurring. In order to better understand the difference between these words, we can use the following example, namely: if we are standing on the beach and watching a swimming shark in the sea, it is the shark in the sea that poses a threat to us, while if we swim in the sea, where sharks also swim, then swimming with sharks is a risk for us, associated with, for example, the loss of life.

10 Referred to in Section 4.4.

11 As an example, use the Global Innovation Index 2020 report (*Global Innovation Index 2020*, GII 2020), which also includes a ranking of the ten most innovative countries of 2020, from the group of low-income economies. It included Tanzania, Rwanda, Nepal, Tajikistan, Uganda, and Burkina Faso. For more on this, see Dutta, et al., 2020.

12 As *argumentum a contrario*, several factors can be pointed out that limit the development of digitization, and which have been characterized in detail – in the form of paradoxes, including strategic, supply chain, talent, innovation, and the physical-digital-physical loop – in a report published in 2018 by Deloitte: *The Industry 4.0 Paradox: Overcoming Disconnects on the Path to Digital Transformation (Deloitte, 2018)*.

13 For more on this topic, see Śledziewska and Włoch, 2020.

14 Digital economy is a term used by Don Tapscott. For more on this, see Tapscott, 1998.

15 For more on this, see Section1.3.

16 Blockchain, in the real world, appeared at the turn of 2016/2017. In a computer network, it is based on a P2P communication model (peer-to-peer, each with each), which means that each user has the same, i.e., equivalent, permissions. Blockchain is a distributed ledger (database) technology that is used to globally record information on a large number of servers and that can be operated simultaneously by many entities in near real time. Its appearance has permanently revolutionized the way various types of records are created, stored, and updated.

17 A due diligence procedure, most often used – but not only – in financial institutions, which allows proper verification of the identity of a given customer.

18 It is a procedure for identifying, verifying, and reviewing data held by an organization, which aims to better understand and understand it. Some types of information at an organization's disposal can serve all stakeholders, while others must remain for its private insight.

19 See Section 2.5.

20 5V symbol – used in characterizing the big-data environment.

21 The Gartner Research Institute (www.gartner.com) reports that by 2021, nearly 80% of business processes in organizations had been modernized and adapted to the requirements related to big data.

22 For more on this, see Jørgensen, 2019.

23 For more on this topic, see *Logistics Market in Europe 2020-2024*, TechNavio, May 2020.

24 Distributed ledger technology (DLT) is a distributed database that is not located in one place but is distributed among a large number of computers on the network. Its members – depending on the permissions granted to them - have both the ability to download and upload data.

Conclusion

The logistics audit is a new and relatively little-described issue in the scientific literature devoted to management, as well as to general audit. A good exemplification of this statement may be the fact that the bibliometric analysis carried out by the authors during the writing of this book – based on the Web of Science (WoS) and Scopus databases – showed that the number of scientific (peer-reviewed) articles containing the phrase "logistics audit" did not exceed 32 in total. What's more, as many as five articles referring to the subject of logistics audit were published only in 2020, while the rest fell in earlier years. However, a clearly greater "wealth" of publications related to logistics audit can be observed in the Google Scholar database. Nevertheless, it is a tool that to this day causes a lot of controversy and gives rise to a lot of divisions in the academic community when it comes to its quality and scientific credibility. However, apart from this, we can conclude, without a shadow of a doubt, that the current knowledge about logistics audit is mainly within journalism publications rather than the scientific literature. It is industry reports, journalistic articles, or specialized Internet blogs, which are often run by people professionally involved in logistics consulting, that provide us with knowledge about what it is, how it works, how it is carried out, and what value this type of audit brings to the organization. Therefore, the knowledge accumulated in this way should become the subject of in-depth analysis by researchers interested not only in the issue of logistics audit or logistics, but also in many other related fields and disciplines. Taking into account the above analysis, the authors believe that the contents of this book will make an important contribution to the development of scientific knowledge about the logistics audit, and internal audit in general, and that they will also meet with a favorable reception from practitioners; particularly because combining scientific knowledge with practice allows for the permanent development of competences, which, in the field of business – but also of science – are considered a *sine qua non* for professional success.

References

Abt, S. (1998). *Zarządzanie logistyczne w przedsiębiorst wie*. Warszawa: Polskie Wydawnictwo Ekonomiczne.

Adamczewski, P. (2018). Ku dojrzałości cyfrowej organizacji inteligentnych. *Studia i Prace Kolegium Zarządzania i Finansów SGH, Zeszyt Naukowy, 161*. Warszawa: Oficyna Wydawnicza SGH.

Adamiecki, K. (1985). *O nauce organizacji*. Warszawa: Polskie Wydawnictwo Ekonomiczne.

Aliyu, A. U. L. (2019). Factors responsible for low productivity in an organization. *International Journal of Economics and Business, 3*(2), ISSN: 2717–3151, LIGS University Hawaii, USA.

Altkorn, J. (2004). *Podstawy marketingu*. Kraków: Instytut Marketingu.

Andjelkovic, A., & Radosavljevic, M. (2020). The length of the distribution channel as a factor of its efficiency. *Strategic Management, 25*(2), 9–017. https://doi.org /10.5937/ StraMan2002009A.

Anthony, R. N., Dearden, J., & Bedford, N. M. (1989). *Management control systems*. Homewood: Irwin.

Antoszkiewicz, J. D. (1999). *Metody heurystyczne. Twórcze rozwiązywanie problemów*. Warszawa: Wydawnictwo Poltext.

Arnold, J., Chapman, S., & Clive, L. (2008). *Introduction to materials management*, wyd. 6. Upper Saddle River, NJ: Pearson Education.

Barcik, R., & Jakubiec, M. (2011). Systemy logistyczne – podstawy funkcjonowania. *Logistyka, 4*, 74–79.

Bartholdi, J. J., & Hackman, S. T. (2006). *Warehouse and distribution science*. www .wareho-. Retrieved from use-science.com.

Bekefi, T., Epstein, J. M., & Yuthas, K. (2008). *Managing opportunities and risks. Management accounting guidelines*. The Society of Management Accountants of Canada, The American Institute of Certified Public Accountants and The Chartered Institute of Management Accountants, Mississaug–New York–London.

Bielińska-Dusza, E. (2009). Identyfikacja problemów badawczych w audycie wewnętrznym. *Zeszyty Naukowe Uniwersytetu Szczecińskiego. Studia i Prace Wydziału Nauk Ekonomicznych i Zarządzania, 16*, 21–35.

Bielińska-Dusza, E. (2011). Funkcjonowanie kontroli zarządczej w systemie kontroli w systemie kontroli wewnętrznej przedsiębiorstwa. *Zeszyty Naukowe Uniwersytetu Szczecińskiego, 669*, 33–48.

Blaik, P. (2001). *Logistyka. Koncepcja zintegrowanego zarządzania.* Warszawa: Polskie Wydawnictwo Ekonomiczne.

Brzeziński, M. (2005). *Logistyka wojskowa.* Dom Wydawniczy. Warszawa: Bellona.

Buła, P. (2015a). *System zarządzania ryzykiem w przedsiębiorstwie, jako element nadzoru korporacyjnego.* Kraków: Wydawnictwo Uniwersytetu Jagiellońskiego.

Buła, P. (2015b). The role of internal audit within corporate risk management viewed from the perspective of corporate governance function. In J. Teczke, K. Djakelii & P. Buła (Eds.), *Management science during destabilization: Local insight* (pp. 285–291). Cracow–Tibilisi: Cracow Univeristy of Economics.

Buła, P., & Niedzielski, B. (2021). *Management, organisations and artificial intelligence. Where theory meets practice.* London: Routledge.

Burke, B. (2020). *Top strategic technology trends for 2021.* Gartner, eBook, Stamfod USA.

Cambalikova, A., & Misun, J. (2017). *The importance of control in managerial work.* International Conference Socio-Economic Perspectives in the Age of XXI century Globalization (pp. 218–229). University of Tirana, Faculty of Economy, Department of Economics, Tirana.

Chow, D., & Heaver, T. (1999). *Logistics strategies for North America* (3rd ed.). Global Logistics and Distribution Planning, Routledge, New York.

Costello, P. J. (2003). Auditing concepts and standards. *NPMA, 15*(6). Atlanta, 12–14.

Cyfert, S. (2006). *Strategiczne doskonalenie architektury procesów w zarządzaniu przedsiębiorstwem.* Poznań: Wydawnictwo Akademii Ekonomicznej w Poznaniu.

Czachorowski, S. (2010). Między ewolucjonizmem a kreacjonizmem – model maszyny i model organizmu. In E. Wiszowaty & K. Parzych-Blakiewicz (Eds.), *Teoria ewolucji a wiara chrześcijan* (s. 60–78). Olsztyn: Wydawnictwo Uniwersytetu Warmińsko-Mazurskiego w Olsztynie.

Dai, J., & Vasarhelyi, M. A. (2016). Imagineering audit 4.0. *Journal of Emerging Technologies in Accounting, 13*(1), 1–15.

De Koster, R. B. M., & Smidts, A. (2013). Organizing warehouse management. *International Journal of Operations and Production Management, 33*(9). https://doi.org/10.1108/ IJOPM-12-2011-0471.

Deloitte. (2018). *The industry 4.0 paradox overcoming disconnects on the path to digital transformation.* Deloitte Touche Tohmatsu Limited.

Dendera-Gruszka, M., Kulińska, E., & Masłowski, D. (2017). Budowa rejestru ryzyka z wy- korzystaniem audytu logistycznego. *Przedsiębiorczość i Zarządzanie*, Wydawnictwo SAN, ISSN 2543-8190, t. XVIII, z. 8, cz. 2, Łódź–Warszawa.

Domschke, W., & Schild, B. (1994). Standortentscheidungen in Distributionssystemen. In H. von Isermann (Ed.), *Logistik – Beschaffung, Produktion, Distribution.* Landsberg am Lech, Köln.

Douglas, M. L. (2008). *An executive summay of supply chain management: Processes, partnerships, performance*. Sarasota, FL: Supply Chain Management Institute, San Diego.

Duda, S. (1997). Typy produkcji w koncepcji Władysława Zawadzkiego. *Annales Universitatis Mariae Curie-Skłodowska, Sectio H, Oeconomia, 31*, 25–49.

Dutta, S., Lanvin, B., & Wunsch-Vincent, S. (2020). *The global innovation index 2020: Who will finance innovation?* NY: Cornell University, INSEAD, World Intellectual Property Organization.

Emerald Publishing Limited. (1988). How do we monitor and report on logistics systems performance? *International Journal of Physical Distribution & Materials Management, 18*(2–3), 78–82. https://doi.org/10.1108/eb014691.

Gary, I., & Manson, S. (2008). *The audit process: Principles, practice and cases* (4th ed.). London: Thomson Learning.

Gattorna, J., Day, A., & Hargreaves, J. (1991). Effective logistics management, *Logistics Information Management, 4*(2). MCB University Press Limited, 2–86.

Gołembska, E. (2007a). *Kompendium wiedzy o logistyce*. Warszawa: Polskie Wydawnictwo Ekonomiczne.

Gołembska, E. (2007b). *Podstawowe problemy logistyki globalnej, międzynarodowej, eurologistyki*. Łódź: Wydawnictwo Naukowe Wyższej Szkoły Kupieckiej.

Gołembska, E. (2010). *Kompendium wiedzy o logistyce* (4th ed.). Warszawa: Wydawnictwo Naukowe PWN.

Gudehus, T., & Kotzab, H. (2012). *Comprehensive logistics*. Berlin–Heidelberg: Springer–Verlag.

Handfield, R. (2020). *What is supply chain management (SCM)?* Raleigh: NC State University.

Handfield, R. B., & Nicols, Jr. E. L., (2002). *Supply chain redesign*. NJ: Prentice Hall, Upper Saddle River, NJ, USA.

Herath, S. K. (2007). A framework for management control research. *Journal of Management Development, 26*(9), 895–915.

Hermanson, D. R., Ivancevich, D. M., & Ivancevich, S. H. (2008). Building an effective internal audit function: Learning from SOX Section 404 reports. *Review of Business, 28*(2), 13–28.

Hochmuth, Ch. A., Bartodziej, Ch., & Schwägler, C. (2017). *Industry 4.0: Is your ERP system ready for digital era?*. https://doi.org/10.13140/RG.2.2.17725.08169.

Ionescu, L. (2010). Exercitarea controlului intern în conditiile crizei economice internationale, Contabilitatea. *expertiza si auditul afacerilor*, nr 8, 55.

Jenkins, B. (1992). *Different types of audits. Environmental auditing in South Australia: Costs and benefits*. https://doi.org/10.13140/RG.2.2.23066.26560.

Jezierski, A. (2007a). Audyt logistyczny w procesach gospodarczych (cz. 1). *Logistyka, 5*, 91–93.

Jezierski, A. (2007b). Audyt logistyczny w procesach gospodarczych (cz. 2). *Logistyka, 6*, 79–82.

Jørgensen, T. (2019). *Digital skills. Where universities matter. Learning and teaching paper #7*. Brussels–Geneva: European University Association.

Kaczmarek, B. (2016). Problemy w organizacji: techniki definiowania problemu. *Ekonomiczne Problemy Usług, 122*, 269–278.

Khan, F. (2018). *Understanding the impact of technology in audit and finance.* London: The Institute of Chartered Accountants in England and Wales, The Dubai Financial Services Authority.

Kisperska-Moroń, D., & Krzyżaniak, S. (2009). *Logistyka.* Poznań: Wydawnictwo ILIM.

Klein, S. (2018). *Logistics audit identifying fields of action to optimize service, quality and costs.* Frankfurt am Main: Miebach Consulting White Paper.

Klug, F. (2018). *Logistikmanagement in Automobilindustrie. Grundlagen der Logistik im Automobilbau.* Berlin: Springer.

Kotler, P., et al. (2010). *Marketing management.* New York: Prentice Hall.

Kowalczyk, L. (2015). Logistics supply as an element of logistic infrastructure in gastronomy on selected example. *Journal of Translogistics.* Wrocław, 139–155.

Kozina, A. (2014). Coalition strategy in (multiparty) negotiations. *Zeszyty Naukowe Uniwersytetu Ekonomiczno-Przyrodniczego w Siedlcach, Seria: Administracja i Zarządzanie, 100*, 67–82.

Krawczyk, S. (2000). *Logistyka w zarządzaniu marketingiem.* Wrocław: Wydawnictwo Akademii Ekonomicznej.

Krzyżaniak, S., Niemczyk, A., Majewski, J., & Andrzejczyk, P. (2014). *Organizacja i monitorowanie procesów magazynowych* (2nd ed.). Poznań: Instytut Logistyki i Magazynowania (ILiM).

Krzyżanowski, L. (1994). *Podstawy nauk o organizacji i zarządzaniu* (2nd ed.). Warszawa: Wydawnictwo Naukowe PWN.

Kulińska, E., & Koziarska, A. (2017). Significance and impact of outsourcing of logistics processes – Case study. *Econometrics, 1*(55). The Univeristy of Technology in Opole. https://doi.org/10.15611/ekt.2017.1.07.

Kupisiewicz, Cz. (1964). *O efektívnosti problémového vyučovania.* Bratislava: SPN.

Lancioni, R. (1991). Distribution cost accounting in international logistics. *International Journal of Physical Distribution and Logistics Management, 21*(8), 12–16.

Langley, G. J., Nolan, K. M., Nolan, T. W., Norman, C. L., & Provost, L. P. (1996). *The improvement guide.* San Francisco: Jossey-Bass Publishers.

Larina, P. P. (2005). *Logistics: Textbook.* Donetsk: Era.

Lee, J., Bagheri, B., Kao, H. A., & Lapira, E. (2015). Industry 4.0 and manufacturing transformation. *Manufacturing Leadership Journal, Vol. 4.*

Linhart, J. (1976). *Činnost a poznávání.* Praha: Academia.

Lisiński, M. (2011). *Audyt wewnętrzny w doskonaleniu instytucji.* Warszawa: Polskie Wydawnictwo Ekonomiczne.

Łobejko, S. (2018). *Strategie cyfryzacji przedsiębiorstw,* t. 2, Materiały konferencyjne, XXI Konferencja Innowacje w Zarządzaniu i Inżynierii, Polskie Towarzystwo Zarządzania Produkcją, Zakopane.

Lwowski, B., & Kozłowski, R. (2007). *Podstawowe zagadnienia zarządzania produkcją.* Kraków: Oficyna Ekonomiczna.

Lysons, K. (2004). *Zakupy zaopatrzeniowe*. Warszawa: Polskie Wydawnictwo Ekonomiczne.

Malindžák, D., Kačmáry, P., Ostasz, G., Gazda, A., Zatwarnicka-Madura, B., & Lorek, M. (2015). *Design of logistic systems. Theory and applications*. New York: Open Science Publishers.

Mastalerz-Kodzis, A. (2018). Methodology of the measurement of territorial unit and organization economical potencial. *Scientific Papers of Silesian University of Technology, Organization and Management Series, 127*, 125–134.

Mazzone, D. M. (2014). *Digital or death: Digital transformation: The only choice for business to survive smash and conquer*. Smashbox Consulting Inc, Ontario.

Merchant, K. A. (1985). *Control in business organizations*. Boston: Pitman.

Meuldijk, M. (2017). Impact of digitization on the audit profession. *Audit Committee News*, Edition 58, Q3 2017, KPMG AG.

Młodzik, E. (2013). Identyfikacja ryzyka – kluczowy element procesu zarządzania ryzykiem w jednostkach gospodarczych. *Zeszyty Naukowe Uniwersytetu Szczecińskiego, 61*, Wydawnictwo Uniwersytetu Szczecińskiego, Szczecin.

Montgomery, R. H. (1956). *Dicksee's auditing. CPA handbook*. Durham: American Institute of Certified Public Accountants.

Mroczko, F. (2016). *Logistyka*. Prace Naukowe Wyższej Szkoły Zarządzania i Przedsiębiorczości. Seria: Zarządzanie, 46. Wałbrzych.

Mynarski, S. (1979). *Elementy teorii systemów i cybernetyki*. Warszawa: Państwowe Wydawnictwo Naukowe.

Nassab, S. G. H. H., Shenass, M. R. K., Aramesh, P., & Nasab, S. M. H. (2013). The effect of production management on increase productivity operations management of Shahid Hashemi Nejad Gas Refinery (Khangiran). *European Online Journal of Natural and Social Sciences, 2*(3), Special Issue on Accounting and Management, 2827–2838.

Nasta, L. N., & Ladar, C. T. (2015). Convergences and divergences between internal and external audit on international context. *AGORA International Journal of Administration Sciences, 1*, 46–55.

Nogalski, B., & Marcinkiewicz, H. (2004). *Zarządzanie antykryzysowe przedsiębiorstwem. Pokonać kryzys i wygrać*. Warszawa: Difin.

Norman, M. (2009). *A look into the future: The next evolution of internal audit continuous risk and control assurance*. Germany: SAP AG.

Nosal, Cz. (1993). *Umysł menedżera*. Wrocław: Wrocławskie Wydawnictwo Przecinek.

Nowakowska, A. (2019). Managing distribution processes in the selected sales. *Network World Scientific News, 123*, 234–245.

Nowicka-Skowron, M. (2000). *Efektywność systemów logistycznych*. Warszawa: Polskie Wydawnictwo Ekonomiczne.

Oklander, M. A. (2005). *Logistics: Textbook*. Kiev: Foreign Trade.

Pająk, W. (2008). Audyt organizacji systemu logistycznego przedsiębiorstwa w procesie tworzenia zintegrowanego łańcucha dostaw. *Zeszyty Naukowe, 774*, 69–83.

Penc, J. (2007). *Leksykon biznesu*. Warszawa: Agencja Wydawnicza Placet.

Petrascu, D. (2010). Internal audit: Defining, objectives, functions and stages. *Studies in Business and Economics, 5*(3). Lucian Blaga University of Sibiu, Faculty of Economic Sciences, 238–246 .

Pfohl, H. Ch. (1998). *Zarządzanie logistyką*. Poznań: ILiM.

Pienaar, W. (2009). *Introduction to business logistics*. Cape Town: Oxford University.

Pieriegud, J. (2016). Cyfryzacja gospodarki i społeczeństwa – wymiar globalny, europejski i krajowy. In J. Gajewski, W. Paprocki & J. Pieriegud (Eds.), *Cyfryzacja gospodarki i społeczeństwa. Szanse i wyzwania dla sektorów infrastrukturalnych* (pp. 11–13). Gdańsk: Instytut Badań nad Gospodarką Rynkową – Gdańska Akademia Bankowa.

Pop, A., Bota-Avram, C., & Bota-Avram, F. (2008). The relationship between internal and external audit. *Annales Universitatis Apulensis Series Oeconomica, 1*(10), 18.

PwC. (2019). *Transport Przyszłości. Raport o perspektywach rozwoju transportu drogowego w Polsce w latach 2020–2030*. Warszawa, PWC project.

Razik, M., Radi, B., & Okar, Ch. (2017). Development of a maturity model for the warehousing function in Moroccan companies. *International Journal of Engineering and Technology (IJET), 9*(2), 280–290. https://doi.org/10.21817/ijet/2017/v9i1/170902303.

Roland Berger Strategy Consultants GmbH. (2015). *The digital transformation of industry. How important is it? Who are the winners? What must be done now?* München, Germany.

RSM International Association. (2019). *Internal audit – The changing landscape*. Mumbai, India: RSM Astute Consulting Pvt. Ltd.

Rut, J., & Miłasiewicz, B. (2016). Logistyka procesu magazynowania w wybranym przedsiębiorstwie – studium przypadku. *Gospodarka Materiałowa i Logistyka, 9,* 24–30.

Satka, E. (2017). Internal and external audit in the function of the management of the trade companies. *Journal of US-China Public Administration, 14*(6), 330–338. https://doi.org/10.17265/1548–6591/2017.06.004.

Savić, D. (2019). From digitization, through digitalization, to digital transformation. January/February, *Online Searcher*, 36–39.

Sawyer, B. L., Dittenhofer, A. M., & Scheiner, H. J. (2003). *Sawyer's internal auditing. 5th edition. The practice of modern internal auditing*. Altamonte Springs, FL: The Institute of Internal Auditors.

Skrzypek, A. (2014). Qualitative aspects of the improvement of the organization's management. *Zeszyty Naukowe Uniwersytetu Przyrodniczo-Humanistycznego w Siedlcach, Seria: Administracja i Zarządzanie, 100,* 131–146.

Skuza, Z. (2019). Selected aspects of supply logistics in the analyzed enterprise. *Gospodarka Materiałowa i Logistyka, 11,* t. LXXI. https://doi.org/10.33226/1231-2037.2019.11.1.

Śledziewska, K., & Włoch, R. (2020). *Gospodarka cyfrowa. Jak nowe technologie zmieniają świat*. Warszawa: Wydawnictwa Uniwersytetu Warszawskiego.

Śliżewska, J., & Zadrożna, D. (2014). *Organizowanie i monitorowanie dystrybucji. Kwalifikacja A.30.3.* Warszawa: Wydawnictwa Szkolne i Pedagogiczne.

Sljivic, S., Skorup, S., & Vukadinovic, P. (2015). Management control in modern organizations. *International Review, 3–4.* https://doi.org/10.5937/intrev1504039S.

Słowiński, B. (2008). *Wprowadzenie do logistyki.* Koszalin: Wydawnictwo Uczelniane Politechniki Koszalińskiej.

Statistics Poland. (2020). *Materials management in 2019. Statistical analyses.* Warsaw, November, Warsaw, Poland.

Sungurtekin, T. (2011). *How a logistics audit can identify bottlenecks and improvements for organizations.* Retrieved from http://EzineArticles.com/.

Swinkels, W. H. A. (2012). *Exploration of a theory of internal audit: A study on the theoretical foundations of internal audit in relation to the nature and the control systems of Dutch public listed firms.* Delft: Eburon.

Szczepańska, K. (2011). *Zarządzanie jakością. W dążeniu do doskonałości.* Warszawa: Wydawnictwo C.H. Beck.

Szklarski, L., & Kozioł, R. (1980). *Systemy sterowania procesem technologicznym w górnictwie.* Warszawa–Kraków: Państwowe Wydawnictwo Naukowe.

Szymonik, A. (2014). Ryzyko w systemach logistycznych. *Zeszyty Naukowe Politechniki Łódzkiej, Seria: Organizacja i Zarządzanie, 1193,* z 58.

Tannenbaum, A. S. (1962). Control in organizations: Individual adjustment and organizational performance. *Administrative Science Quarterly, 7*(2), 236–257.

Tapscott, D. (1998). *Gospodarka cyfrowa. Nadzieje i niepokoje Ery Świadomości Systemowej.* Warszawa: Business Press.

Testa, M. R., & Sipe, J. L. (2013). The organizational culture audit: Countering cultural ambiguity in the service context. *Open Journal of Leadership, 2*(2), 36–44. https://doi.org/10.4236/ojl.2013.22005.

The Institute of Internal Auditors. (2016). *All in day's work a look at the varied responsibilities of internal auditors,* No. 10. United States: Global Headquarters.

Trenkner, M. (2016). Doskonalenie procesów i ich uwarunkowania. *Journal of Management and Finance, 14*(2–1), 429–438.

Twaróg, J. (2003). *Mierniki i wskaźniki logistyczne.* Poznań: ILiM.

Voortman, C. (2004). *Global logistics management.* Cape Town: Juta and Co Ltd.

Wąchol, J. (2010). Nowoczesne instrumenty zarządzania a nadzór korporacyjny. *Zeszyty Naukowe Uniwersytetu Szczecińskiego. Studia Informatica, 26,* 155–165.

Wasiak, M. (2013). Uwarunkowania stosowania systemu logistycznego do optymalizacji potencjałów systemów przewozowych. *Logistyka, 4,* 757–768.

Wawrzynowicz, J., & Wajszczuk, K. (2012). *The model of logistics audit for agricultural enterprises.* In Proceedings of the Carpathian Logistics Congress, 7–9 November. Jesenik: Czech Republic.

Żebrucki, Z. (2012). Rola audytu w usprawnianiu systemu logistycznego przedsiębiorstwa. Zeszyty Naukowe Politechniki Śląskiej: Organizacja i Zarządzanie, vol. 60, pp. 421–433.

Ziyadin, S., Suieubayeva, S., & Utegenova, A. (2020). Digital transformation in business. In S. Ashmarina, M. Vochozka & V. Mantulenko (Eds.), *Digital age: Chances, challenges and future. ISCDTE 2019.* Lecture Notes in Networks and

Systems, vol 84. Cham: Springer. https://doi.org/10.1007/978-3-030-27015-5 _49.

Žofková, M., & Drábek, J. (2019). *Application of innovative approaches in enterprise management based on the logistic audit*. 11th International Scientific Conference Economics, Management and Technology in Enterprises 2019 (EMT 2019). Advances in Economics, Business and Management Research, 78.ww

Index

Note: Page locators in italics refer to figures and bold refer to tables.

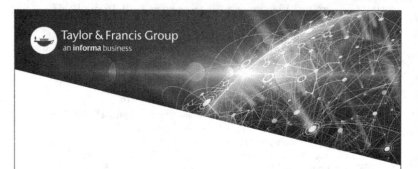

Printed in the United States
by Baker & Taylor Publisher Services